Engaging Motherhood

Heart Preparation for a Holy Calling

Holly Mackle and Linda Barrett

© 2016 - Committee on Discipleship Ministries
1700 North Brown Road, Suite 102
Lawrenceville, Georgia 30043
Bookstore: 1-800-283-1357
678-825-1100
www.pcacdm.org/bookstore

All rights reserved. No part of this book may be reproduced, stored in a retrieval system, or transmitted in any form or by any means—electronically, mechanical, photocopy, recording, or otherwise—excerpted as expressly allowed herein or for brief quotations for the purpose of review or comment, without the prior permission of the publisher, Committee on Discipleship Ministries, at the above address.

The Holy Bible, English Standard Version™ Copyright © 2000; 2001 by Crossway Bibles, A Division of Good News Publishers, 1300 Crescent Street, Wheaton, Illinois 60187, USA. All Rights Reserved.

This edition published by arrangement with Crossway Bibles, a Division of Good News Publishers. *The Holy Bible, English Standard Version*™ is adapted from the *Revised Standard Version* of the Bible, copyright Division of Christian Education of the National Council of Churches of Christ in the USA. All Rights Reserved.

Cover design by Selena Fettig with artwork used from www.createthecut.com

Database(C) 2001 iExalt, Inc.

ISBN: 978-1-944964-02-3

Dear mommy,

That's exciting, isn't it! Being called mommy. It's the most wonderful feeling in all the world. It conjures up images of tender moments cuddling your little one, kissing boo-boos, or picking up a sweetly smiling toddler. What nobody mentions is that you're cuddling because it's 4 a.m. and they have been screaming since just after midnight, that boo-boo is a goose egg of questionable size that makes you wonder if you should head to the ER, and you're grabbing the toddler to keep them from sticking their hands into the toilet bowl. If I had a nickel for every time a stranger said to me, "Enjoy every moment! They grow up so fast!" Sometimes I'm tempted to answer, "So I hear, but could you hold this one for five minutes so I could go to the bathroom by myself?"

It really is good, exciting and sweet. But not all the time. Sometimes it's just plain hard. Or dare I say, sometimes it's just not what you expected. This study was written by moms with a heart for women taking that plunge into motherhood for the first time, the fourth time, or just weary with the four year old. While the voices and writing styles are different, we hope you will see that the heart is very much the same. Our experiences differ only in specifics—the answer to our deepest longings, our greatest fears, or our unmet expectations has always been the same: Jesus.

The good days are *great*. Drink them in. Take pictures. Rock a little bit longer. Tickle that toddler one more time, or read just one more book than you planned. Rejoice and give thanks to a loving God who created motherhood for you! Who formed your child—natural or adopted—to be yours and nobody else's. Who saw fit for humankind to love one another in the context of family. But when the hard days come, and they will, our prayer is that you will run to the loving and merciful Abba Father.

The purpose of this study is to help you be better prepared for the not-so-good days. For the days when sin flares up, expectations go unmet, and relationships are strained. We hope you will find in these pages a thoughtful and prayerful preparation for the ups and downs of motherhood. We hope this material will help you develop habits that will serve you well once your little one arrives, or that will encourage you when you can't seem to find a quiet spot in your own house. We hope you will be calmed and steadied by the experiences of some women who have gone down this road before you.

The study is composed of eight weeks—the first week to meet the other moms and your facilitator(s), and the latter seven weeks for the actual study. Each week, there are 5 short devotionals as preparation for the time with your group. The weeks are topical, and the theme that you see in the devotional days will be further explored in your group setting. Additionally, there is a special section in the back for moms that have come to motherhood through other paths, with a special focus on the adoptive mom. We hope that the Holy Spirit will guide and prompt your thoughts and prayers throughout the day toward the topic at hand. There is no better preparation than prayer for a day spent nurturing little lives. Run to the God who cares for you—to the God who will "gently lead those that are with young" (Isaiah 40:11). We hope you will find comfort, peace and sisterhood in these pages.

All glory be unto King Jesus.

With love,

Holly, Linda, Jenn, Jessica, and Brandie

Table of Contents

Welcome 3

WEEK ONE—Meet and Greet

    Group Member Info 11

WEEK TWO—Role Change *(Dr. Jenn Hale)* 13

    Revolution. 13

    Marriage Metamorphosis. 15

    A New Career. 18

    The Fire of Friendship 20

    Your Delivery. 22

WEEK THREE—Control *(Holly Mackle)* 25

    She Blooms. 25

    Today and Forever 27

    A Stinging Realization 29

    Equipped 31

    "Wake Up, Jesus!". 33

WEEK FOUR—Perfectionism *(Holly Mackle)*. 35

    Supermom vs. Not-So-Much. 35

    Just as We Are. 37

    No Accident. 39

    A Night Out. 41

    Not My Will. 43

WEEK FIVE—Comparison *(Jessica B. Hale)* 45

    Whom Am I Following? 45

    Liberty from Measuring Up. 47

    Looking for Answers? 49

    New Mercies. 51

    Living in the Gray 53

WEEK SIX—Loneliness *(Brandie Wolfe)* 57

    So Alone. 57

    Isolation for the Stay-at-Home-Mom 59

    Isolation for the Working Mom. 61

    Illness 63

    Community. 65

WEEK SEVEN—Expecting Emotions *(Linda Barrett)* . . 67

    In the Image of God 67

    Gratitude vs. Anger 69

    Hope vs. Fear 71

    Joy vs. Sorrow. 73

    How Do I Get There? Confidence in Christ 75

WEEK EIGHT—Spiritual Life After Baby Arrives
(Linda Barrett). 79

    Help Me to Never Forget! 79

    One Thing Necessary 81

    Eyes Wide Open 83

    All of Life. 85

    Overflowing Grace. 87

NO CONDEMNATION: A Mother's Day Sermon
(Matt Redmond) 89

**ADDITIONAL ENCOURAGEMENT FOR THE
ADOPTIVE MOM**
(Carrie Brock and Lauren Kirkland) 93

For David. Life is good in all directions. (HM)

To God, family, and friends: all inspired my thoughts and created an ache for grace. (LB)

To my incredible mother, Karen Byers, and my own two beautiful daughters, Aliena and Emaleigh. (JMH)

To the Lord, for opening my eyes to grace; to Justin, for giving me courage to risk and write. (JBH)

For my two arrows and my husband, who loved me through every wavering emotion. (BW)

To my three precious and unexpected gifts from God. You were worth the wait. (CB)

All praise to Jehovah Rapha, who healed my heart through adoption and gave us our precious boys. (LK)

Acknowledgements

The writers would like to thank Melany Guzzo and Keri Adams, whose hearts, many years ago, conceptualized a way to love women in the hard early days of mothering. Transforming the concept into the idea of a study was the work of Mary Williams Branch, who has supported us, loved us, and encouraged our kingdom eyes. We are grateful to Dr. Stephen Estock and CDM for believing in our project, and to Greg Poole, heresy-checker extraordinaire. We want to thank Cara Johnson for her astute editorial eye and for guiding the first group through this study. Not a page of this work is unaffected by the way she loves Jesus. Catherine Chestnut, Libby Minor, and Cammie Schrimsher were all invaluable first draft readers and editors, and we are grateful for their thoughtful contributions. Finally, we are who we are because of the deep gospel work springing up from the aircraft carrier that is Oak Mountain Presbyterian Church. May many come to taste grace and walk in freedom as a result of the faithful teaching of its pastors and authentic fellowship of its body.

Week One

First Meeting

Who's in My Group

My Facilitator is _____

Phone # _____

My Facilitator is _____

Phone # _____

Name _____

Phone # _____

Address _____

Expecting a/some _____

Due Date _____

Name _____

Phone # _____

Address _____

Expecting a/some _____

Due Date _____

Name _____

Phone # _____

Address _____

Expecting a/some _____

Due Date _____

Name _____

Phone # _____

Address _____

Expecting a/some _____

Due Date _____

Name _____

Phone # _____

Address _____

Expecting a/some _____

Due Date _____

Week Two

Role Change

Day 1:
Revolution

*"Who, though he was in the form of God, did not count
equality with God a thing to be grasped,
but emptied himself, by taking the form of a servant."*
Philippians 2:6-7

Tick, tock. Your weeks, months, maybe even years of waiting are almost over. Your baby is just hours (even if it is a few hundred) away from turning your world upside down. From rearranging what feels like your whole life. From ushering in a new era of beauty and responsibility. The car seat has been installed, your bags packed. The nursery finished. But you... you're not sure you're really ready. Regardless, the revolution is near.

But what if I told you there was a great High Priest who has gone before you and knows all your fears? What if I told you that Christ has taken the lion's share of your pain in delivery? By leaving his throne in heaven and taking on the very nature of a man—a servant—Jesus embraced the most astronomical role change you could ever imagine. God became man with flesh and bones and bruises. And his earthly body was torn open to deliver you. And because of this, God exalted him to the highest place, so that at the name of Jesus every knee would bow. If you have confessed Christ as Lord, you can have the unwavering hope that God will deliver you into this revolution with joy and confidence.

So in reality, this tiny new life will not turn your world upside down—it will set everything right again. When a baby arrives, you will be birthed yourself through pain into this wonderful, tearful, sweet, fierce, protective, loving role of a mother. In many ways, it is the very pinnacle of self-denial and sacrifice. Your life (needs, desires, schedule, plans) in exchange for your child's. Oh, you will get "yourself" back, in some form. But that's not the point. The point is—if you allow it—becoming a mother can do more to transform you into Christ's likeness than any theology class or Bible study ever could. Why? Because you are walking a path traced out by Jesus Himself. Within the crucible of motherhood we are continually dying to self so another may have life and flourish. Sound familiar? Sacrifice brings life. Self-denial brings blessing. Somehow, through all of this, you become more of who you were created to be. This is the gospel. This is the true revolution of motherhood. And by it we are made new again.

1. **Read Philippians 2:6-11.** Have you trusted in the perfect life of Jesus Christ and his finished work on the cross as payment for your sins? Are there areas in your life where you still remain "on the throne"? What do you think will be the hardest area in which to die?

2. What are some of the ways you hope motherhood will change and grow you into a greater image-bearer of Christ?

Jesus, in my heart I have set apart myself as lord, not you. I have wanted—even fought—to retain control over my life, my body, marriage, career, friendships, everything. I confess this as sin and pray you would deliver me. Amen

Day 2:
Marriage Metamorphosis

"He made streams come out of the rock and caused waters to flow down like rivers."
Psalm 78:16

"We're going to Hawaii no matter what." It was a trip we were hoping to take for our fifth anniversary. "What if you have a baby?" someone asked. "We'll still go," I asserted confidently. "Our marriage comes first. After all, a newborn sleeps all the time and wouldn't even realize we're away."

Fast-forward a few years. I am pregnant with our first daughter, who happens to be due three weeks after our fifth anniversary. What irony. The day she is born, I am filled with a sudden, fierce—and completely unexpected—rush of emotions. I am protective. I am overwhelmed. I am amazed, enamored, overcome. I am in love. And I am taken utterly by surprise. Hawaii? Forget Hawaii!! I don't even want to drive down the street without our daughter. Where did this come from? How did I get here? Where is the old me?

Thankfully, God has a sense of humor. He must have laughed at how confident I had been before becoming a mother. Confident that nothing *really* was going to change. Just another person to think for, right? Looking back, I wasn't prepared for the violent revolution that would take place in my heart with the birth of each of my daughters. And for how my marriage could change (and would change), for the better. From the delivery room to their college dorm and beyond, God, having our best in mind, still calls us as women to place our husbands first if we are married. What does this mean?

Well, it doesn't mean there is a formula. It does mean he can make streams flow out of rocky places. It means he is more than able to see us through the days of motherhood when energy is running low, emotions are running high, dinner needs to be made, and you still need to have that challenging conversation with your husband. It means your marriage can grow richer and fuller as you walk together through these mighty waters of change, clinging to the cross. That he will guide us with a cloud by day and with light from the fire at night. Marriage, when tried in the crucible of child rearing, can emerge purer and more radiant than before. Why? Not because you are committed to your marriage, but because God is committed to your marriage. And he is all you need.

1. What are some of the hopes you have for your marriage with children in the picture? What are your fears? How have your expectations of your marriage changed since you have had children?

Role Change

2. Using the above passage as a guide, how have you seen God work in wondrous ways in your life and marriage? In what ways is God currently calling you to embrace your role as a wife and mother?

God, thank you in advance for leading my husband and me through seasons of change. Enable me to love him sacrificially even when I am exhausted and empty. Fill me up for the purpose of pouring me out. Amen.

Day 3:
A New Career

"She dresses herself with strength and makes her arms strong. She perceives that her merchandise is profitable. Her lamp does not go out at night."
Proverbs 31:17-18

Children leave virtually no area of your life untouched, including your career and home life. Whether you stay at home full-time or continue working (full- or part-time), rest assured God is intimately involved in your life and knows your needs even before (and better than) you do.

Since he is truly a God of infinite possibilities whose thoughts and ways are higher than ours—be aware that his best for you may look different than his best for someone else. He calls some mothers into the workplace and calls others to stay home. Women at both ends of the spectrum—and everywhere in between—have felt judged by others for their position on this issue. Listen carefully for the soft but firm voice of your Maker for his plan for your life. He will speak to your heart. Linger at the foot of the cross. You will find no condemnation there.

So . . . staying home? Run to Jesus. Despite how you may feel, you are not losing your career. You are simply in a new one. Taking care of children is a full-time career for every mother. It requires the very best that you have all the time. Rewards may appear small in the beginning, but you are investing in and cultivating fruit for a lifetime. Use your gifts of creativity, planning, organization, or spontaneity to add beauty and color to your home life. You will have no lack of opportunity, and your family stands to benefit greatly if you submit to God and use your time and talents wisely.

Going back to work full- or part-time? Run to Jesus. His Spirit authored the scriptures, which includes the description of the amazing woman of Proverbs 31. Somehow she finds time for work outside the home (in some capacity) without sacrificing relationships within the home. Difficult decisions will need to be made in light of this new addition to your family. Compromise is unavoidable. You now have two "careers" and less time for other things. But God's heart for you is the same: that you would trust him daily for your needs and respond humbly if his priorities—your relationships at home—are not flourishing. As a working mother, your family, too, stands to benefit greatly if you submit to God and use your time and talents wisely.

1. As you seek God's will regarding your decision to return to work or stay home, what are some of the things you may be tempted to believe? How can you make sure you are looking to Christ to find your identity?

2. God often brings revolution into our lives to show us our need for Him. How does the knowledge that Christ died to bring you liberty actually free you to live radically for Christ as a stay-at-home or working mother?

Lord, I want to follow wherever you are leading me—whether into the workplace as a mother or at home in my new role. Rid me of any feelings of superiority or inferiority, that I may find my identity in you alone.

Day 4:
The Fire of Friendship

"Take care, brothers, lest there be in any of you an evil, unbelieving heart, leading you to fall away from the living God. But exhort one another every day, as long as it is called 'today,' that none of you may be hardened by the deceitfulness of sin."

Hebrews 3:12-13

Have you ever considered that God designed friendships as a primary means of preventing us from being hardened by sin's deceitfulness? The encouragement, challenge, chaffing, sculpting, and sharpening are direct results of true, growing, biblical friendships. Being surrounded by a community of other women does not guarantee a softened heart toward the things of God. Satan is tricky. His wiles are unscrupulous. And sin is relentless. But we are buffered to some extent by the prayers, love, and even discipline of other God-fearing women.

The word "encourage" in Greek means to call near, comfort, exhort, entreat, or pray. God designs friendships for a multitude of purposes, one of which is to call us near. But call us near to what? To the heat radiating from the fire of the gospel. By it we are warmed—sometimes even burned—in order to resurrect and transform our dead, dry, and hardened lives into things of beauty and purpose.

The Lord will place women in your path to walk beside you on this journey of motherhood. Some relationships may deepen as you share new common ground. Some may grow more distant as your time becomes less flexible. However, for your own growth and protection, do not limit your intimate friendships to other mothers. Wisdom has many faces. Perspective and godly counsel transcend age, distance, marital status, career, and personality type.

During my post-graduate years, I was discipled by a woman in my profession who has friends all over the world—women she calls upon for advice, perspective, prayer, and encouragement. She calls them her "panel." Some are single, others are missionaries, a few are similar in age and married with children, one is younger (me), and a few are older. I have the privilege of knowing many of these women—there could not be a more diverse group! But 15 years of friendship have demonstrated the transforming and even sin-defying power of these sweet, gospel-centered relationships.

1. Take inventory of the women in your life. Pray. Is there anyone you feel the Lord leading you to spend more time with as you seek wisdom in motherhood?

2. Are there any single or newly married women you can encourage? Or unbelieving women you can talk with about Jesus? Take time to warm yourself by the fire of relationship. Your heart will melt to the things of God.

God, please surround me with women in all walks of life who can lead me by word or example to the cross. Enable me by your grace to make the most of every—even brief—opportunity. Use me in others' lives to encourage and sharpen them. Amen.

Day 5:
Your Delivery

"Humble yourselves, therefore, under the mighty hand of God so that at the proper time he may exalt you, casting all your anxieties on him, because he cares for you."
1 Peter 5:6-7

Tick, tock. The clock on the mantel chimes "two" and you awake to the sounds of whimpering (or screaming) from the room next door. You quickly pick up your little one and head to the nearest rocking chair, hoping for a fast return to sleep for both of you. Within several minutes, you realize it is not to be. Your little bundle is wide awake and ready to play. You burp her, feed her a little more and before long baby settles in and your thoughts begin to wander to what seems like a previous life.

Once you were at the office giving a presentation wearing high heels and a suit. Or perhaps you were giving your time and energy to teach a classroom of third graders. Or maybe you had been working busily at home, putting the finishing touches on your taxes (and the nursery). But now . . . everything is different. You have gone from having your own space and time, a clean house, regular date nights, and a predictable schedule to . . . what? As the clock on your mantel chimes "three" you realize this creature has ushered in change that has spilled over into every aspect of your life. Your marriage. Your career. Your friendships. Your home. Even your car. The old has been overthrown and the new order has arrived. It is nothing short of a revolution.

Revolution. Have you ever thought about the meaning of that word? "A sudden, complete or marked change in something." It fits, doesn't it? But this is not the first time a tiny baby has caused the world to stop in its tracks. It happened once before, in a dirty stable. And His birth was announced by the angels to a bunch of sleepy shepherds: "Come and worship! The old has been overthrown, the new order has arrived!" So in a way, you are in good company. And if you allow it, this revolution has the power to transform your life, lifting you out of the ordinary and into the throne room of grace where you will find Jesus. And along with Him, everything you need.

So in the middle of the night as you hold your little one, don't stop there. Embrace the overthrow. Because the biggest transformation is really not the baby's birth. It's yours.

Embrace the revolution. Welcome to being a mother.

1. In the midst of this "motherhood revolution," where is the first place you run to for comfort and security?

2. The birth of Christ, his death and resurrection for our sins, ushered in the greatest revolution the world has ever known. How does this reality encourage you in your new role? How does it challenge you?

God, I am so thankful that you have given me the privilege of becoming a mother. Enable me to turn all of my dreams and fears about this revolution over to you. Make me into the women and mother you created me to be. Amen.

Week Three

Control

Day 1:
She Blooms

"Consider the lilies, how they grow:
they neither toil nor spin, yet I tell you, even Solomon
in all his glory was not arrayed like one of these."
Luke 12:27

I might not labor or spin, but I sure do know how to worry. I can fret with the best of them—I can spin possible negative outcomes that would make TV writers beg me to lend them a twist ending. Sometimes, I confess with embarrassment, when a situation is bad enough, worrying at least feels like I'm doing *something*. What do I worry over? The answer is simple enough: everything I can't control and some of the things that I think I can.

Time and time again, Jesus calls people to the unexpected. To the rich young ruler: "Think you love me perfectly? Give it all away and follow me." To the healed demoniac: "Think you want to follow me? No, go and return to your home and your family and tell what I have done for you." To those who had family business to take care of: "Want to go and come back? Let the dead bury the dead." His words are specific to the heart of a situation. So what's mine? Easy enough: "Worry much? Think of the most beautiful flower you can imagine. It does nothing to be that way—it does nothing to create its own beauty and splendor. It simply sits back and *lets it happen*."

That sounds decidedly less busy than I like. Actually, it even sounds a little counterintuitive. Lord, do you not see all this responsibility I have? Do you not see all these people who depend on me, one of whom is dependent on me for *everything*? And how am I ever going to keep all these balls in the air if I stop reeling to rest and trust you? How will my life be full of beauty and splendor *unless I make it that way*?

But look what he calls us to: not to "labor" or "spin," but to rest. To growth that is dependent entirely on him and would not happen apart from him. To beauty and splendor that might look different from what the world would consider splendid. To laying down the idol of control in favor of faith and trust in his goodness. To the life of a wildflower—beautiful and splendid not because of what she did but because her loving creator God made her that way.

1. What is one area of life that I'm constantly struggling to control?

2. Sounds silly, but try it: If you were a wildflower, imagine what you would look like. Imagine how God would delight in your beauty. Reflect on how little you would have to do with creating/dressing/maintaining/being responsible for that beauty.

God, I want to open my controlling hands and choose you. I don't want to fight and struggle for my plan—I want to willingly release mine and trust in yours. Help me today to see and repent of areas where I attempt to control and not trust in you.

Day 2:
Today and Forever

*"Strengthen the weak hands, and make firm the feeble knees.
Say to those who have an anxious heart, 'Be strong; fear not!
Behold, your God will come with vengeance,
with the recompense of God. He will come and save you.'"*

Isaiah 35: 3-4

We have a Savior who is as much coming as he is come. The beautiful yet sometimes excruciating tension of the "now and not yet" can cause us to stumble and to doubt the risen Jesus. I look at my feet and I trip. I look ahead and I walk . . . maybe even gracefully. But this is tricky in the midst of life's ins and outs. While my circumstances shout at me, the truth of who I am as a daughter of the King seems barely a whisper. Is this the battleground of faith? Trusting that what we can't see, taste or touch is the real truth and we are just deceived by the apparent realness of this world?

The not yet of eternity with Jesus is just as true as the struggle to hold his hand in this life. Oh, Lord, may the eternal feel just as real as the worries of the day . . . especially as the worries of the day take on the particularly sensitive prick of wanting to do the right thing in caring for your child.

If possible today, take a few moments to identify what your greatest fears are as you walk in the precise spot of motherhood that you're currently in. As you name each fear, immediately counter it with truth—even write it down if it will help. Afraid that your parenting experience is not going exactly as you had planned before it was a reality? Name God's promises to never leave us or let us go. Fearful that your body may never go back to what it once was? Ask your Creator to allow you to see yourself as he sees you. Wondering if your child is never going to be an A student or a star athlete? Remind yourself that it is God himself who knits us together just as he sees fit. There is power in naming fear and bringing it before the feet of a loving and caring Abba Father.

He won't let it stand—he will destroy it with truth.

1. What do I most worry over now? What is one way I can specifically combat that fear with truth?

2. Why do you think God is so forceful throughout scripture in telling us to "fear not!"?

Abba Father, you want us to call you that because you want us to see you that way—as a caring, loving, protecting daddy. May you be more real to me than my fears today. And when fear does creep in, may I surrender it to you. Please give me the strength to preach truth to myself today and to tell myself to "take heart!"

Day 3:
A Stinging Realization

"Commit your work to the Lord, and your plans will be established. The heart of man plans his way, but the Lord establishes his steps."
Proverbs 16:3, 9

A few years ago, a light bulb went on in my marriage. While on a weekend getaway with some couple friends, we were asked: "What have your biggest marital arguments been about?" As we answered, an embarrassing and unfortunate commonality surfaced: I was afraid. Conflict arose, it tapped into a personal fear over my safety or protection or comfort, and it resulted in an argument. My husband was gracious and compassionate, but the light bulb went on for him, too. I was exposed, and a sin pattern drew its ugly, slithering, slimy path visibly through my history.

Think of a woman you know whom you would characterize as a woman of faith. What attributes does she possess that make you classify her that way? What does she do or not do when she is in a pressure situation? What does her walk with the Lord look like? Whatever you're thinking of, I'm the opposite. I manipulate, plan or arrange my way into ensuring that my circumstances will most likely provide me with safety or comfort. I don't want to be this way. I don't want to rely on anyone or anything but the Lord for my provision and safekeeping. I want to trust the tiniest member of my family to God's perfect and providential will. But when that tiny family member arrives, it's often a whole new ball game, and mama bear can react a little more, let's say, *efficiently* to a situation where she is fearful.

I urge you, and myself, to trust in the Lord. To walk in faith through his perfect plan for your (or my) life. To recognize the slimy paths of sin and to repent of them and be washed clean. May we both, today and every day after this, be a woman that another may characterize as a woman of faith.

Especially if that woman looking on happens to be our own child.

1. Name three attributes of the woman of faith that came to mind.

2. When you are fearful, in what ways can you consider that it is the Lord who truly establishes your plans?

Lord, please guide me in faith today. Help me to see when I am grasping or clawing for control over my life. My life belongs to you alone. Help me to demonstrate my belief with both my heart and my actions.

Day 4:
Equipped

"'My grace is sufficient for you, for my power is made perfect in weakness.' Therefore I will boast all the more gladly of my weaknesses, so that the power of Christ may rest upon me."
2 Corinthians 12:9

"You did not choose me, but I chose you and appointed you that you should go and bear fruit and that your fruit should abide, so that whatever you ask the Father in my name, he may give it to you. These things I command you so that you will love one another."
John 15:16-17

"'And who knows whether you have not come to the kingdom for such a time as this?'"
Mordecai to Esther in Esther 4:14

"Give it a few years, you'll be more suited for motherhood when they're older."

"Nurturing just isn't your thing."

"You're not like her. She's compassionate and maternal. You're just different."

Lies, all lies. Lies I have heard multiple times in the course of my parenting journey, and more importantly, all lies I have believed.

Satan didn't have to feed me much more than this to get his desired result—a disconnected, bored, out-of-place mama, who wondered if she made a terrible life mistake. I viewed my children as energy and independence-drains that needed to be shuffled from activity to activity, place to place, in the most efficient way, so as to keep as much of my own sanity as was humanly possible.

But God is gracious and merciful, and he didn't allow me to stay there for long. He used a small group to reveal my sin patterns, to cause me to grieve the lost months (years?), and to find forgiveness, redemption and change at the cross. Those subtle lies resulted in a belief system that hissed "I don't have what it takes" and encouraged behavior patterns of disengagement from my small children. And God wants to reveal Himself through my being engaged in a beautiful way with them! Scripture teaches us that we have exactly what it takes, for precisely this moment, day, phase, and child, and that if we are in need of any wisdom we simply have to ask. The truth is that he chose ME (and not another mother) to be the mama for these children. I don't have what it takes for my friend's children. I don't what it takes for yours. But I do have what it takes for mine—by his grace and mercy, I've got all the tools in my toolbox.

There is so much power in that! If we really believe this stuff, we can walk into what he's calling us to, right now in this minute! I no longer have to look to some unforeseen future date where I realize "oh, now I'm good at being a mom." It means that my strengths and weaknesses, successes and "failures" are all perfectly suited to what God wants to do in the life of my child, for the purposes of their own sanctification and faith journey, and that He will use them. It means that, thanks be to God, I'm not ultimately in control.

1. I don't think that all women are disengaged from their children, but are you?

2. Name a specific lie that you hear in regard to parenting, and name its consequence. What (or who) suffers when you believe it?

Lord, I want to engage with my children. Show me what stands in the way of that so I may have a repentant heart, and experience the ways in which you want to bring life to my family through me.

Day 5:
"Wake Up, Jesus!"

> *"Then he rose and rebuked the winds and the sea, and there was a great calm. And the men marveled, saying, 'What sort of man is this, that even the winds and sea obey him?'"*
>
> Matthew 8:26-27

In Matthew 8, an exhausted Jesus climbs into a boat with his disciples and immediately falls asleep. The disciples are expecting a calm trip—they are used to this sea, they fish it all the time—but they get anything but calm. An unexpected monster of a storm tosses the boat in such a way that the disciples fear for their lives . . . and Jesus sleeps on.

I can only imagine what the disciples are thinking: "Seriously?" "Doesn't he care about us?" "Has he let us follow him all this way just to die in some freak storm?" If I had been there, there would have been no two ways about it: I would have been just plain mad. Why? Because I had trusted someone enough to leave everyone and everything I knew and to follow him. I had given him control over me, but he wasn't doing what I wanted him to do with that power. Protect me. Care for me in the way I think I need. Do what I want. *Actually, let me be the one in control.*

If you are a follower of Jesus, you are a surrendered one. You have given over control of your life to the Savior. The problem for many believers (including myself), is that it's easy to give over control of one's eternity. Sure I can trust Jesus with something I can't even fathom. But the here and now?

The day-to-day discipline and sleep schedule and quality time with my husband? No thanks, Jesus, I've got this one on my own. And therein lies the deception of control. Christ wants to be a part of our comings and goings, our day ins and day outs. He cares about the play-dates, the baby blues, the rough patches with your own mother; he cares about the calm and the storms.

I love the disciples' reaction "What sort of man is this?" Translation: he's not like me. And that I get, and I want to get at a deeper level every day of my walk with the Lord. We are not the same, he and I. He is God, and I am not. I can act as if I'm in control, but I'm not. He is responsible not just for my eternity, but for my day to days. And should he see fit, he will look at a storm cross-eyed and make it into the calmest and starriest night I've ever seen.

1. Name one specific area you deceive yourself by thinking you have control over.

2. What would it look like to truly surrender that area to Christ's control?

Lord, let me not be deceived. You are God, and I am not. Please help me surrender each part of my day to you, and help me to raise a child who sees a surrendered mommy that delights in your plan for her life.

Week Four

Perfectionism

Day 1:
Supermom Vs. Not–So–Much

"Come to me, all who labor and are heavy laden, and I will give you rest. Take my yoke upon you, and learn from me, for I am gentle and lowly in heart, and you will find rest for your souls."
Matthew 11:28-29

Sometimes the laundry basket is empty. Sometimes my daughter looks cute for preschool. Sometimes my husband walks into a peaceful home, smells a delicious dinner on the stove, and receives a warm reception from his wife. We all remember enough from high school English to realize that the key word here is "sometimes." Because the truth is, sometimes this crazy-motherhood-wifehood-life thing actually works. But if I'm honest with myself, most of the time I'm left wanting in the "Pinterest-worthiness" department. I have found that most women in our generation were brought up to be self-reliant, independent, and confident. Women who can get things done efficiently and pleasantly. Women who were taught from birth that they could accomplish anything . . . *and did.* And now accomplishment looks like making it through a day without spit-up running down the back of your pants leg.

Where do we run when the dishes are piled up, the baby is crying from what you fear may be the fourth ear infection, and the husband has been wearing the same pair of pants for three days running because you keep promising to finish the laundry? And where do we run when *they aren't*. When it's all working . . . maybe even well. There's really no difference. (Well, except for the ear infection part . . . maybe you should get that checked out.) Our hearts are desperate for Christ no matter what our circumstances. When life works, sin flares up, and when life doesn't work—sin still flares up.

Sometimes you will feel like supermom, and sometimes you won't. (Or, what would be more representative of my household is *most of the time* you won't.) And if you're someone who is used to getting things *accomplished* and *checked off* and *neatly tied up*, unfortunately it will soon be time to re-prioritize. I'm so thankful that our Savior doesn't want to be with us on only our good days or only on our bad days. His call is only to come as we are. And motherhood gives the "as you are" a whole different meaning.

1. What aspects of your life have been most painful or difficult to watch your habits change, after adding children to the mix? (housekeeping, quiet nights with your hubby, maintaining friendships?)

2. Spend a moment reflecting on our God who wants to be with us all the time—on both good days and bad.

Father, today may I come to you. No matter what the day holds I pray that I would hear your voice beckoning me to your presence, and I pray that I would respond willingly. Help me to understand that I'm in a stage of life that fluctuates by the moment, and prepare my heart to seek my identity in you and not in my circumstances.

Day 2:
Just As We Are

*"Just as I am, without one plea,
But that thy blood was shed for me,
And that thou bidst me come to thee,
O Lamb of God, I come, I come."*

"Just as I Am," Charlotte Elliott, 1835

Where do you fall in the spectrum of perfectionism? Are you Suzy Do-Right and struggle with finding your worth in your clean house, well-dressed child, and *Gourmet* magazine dinner? Or do you fall on the other end of the spectrum—totally overwhelmed by anything more than getting through the day, so it feels easier to throw your hands up and just let life happen, slightly disgusted by all those women who appear to actually be "trying."

As a teenager I read through the Sermon on the Mount, desperate as a Suzy Do-Right to find ways to please my Savior. The progression of Christ's sermon is fascinating—some of the more comforting and familiar are right up front. But then Jesus goes on to up the conviction. By the end, he's no longer just asking for meekness, mercy or purity, but his actual words are "you therefore must be perfect, as your heavenly Father is perfect." (Matt. 5:48) Brain explosion. Overwhelming dejection. Complete helplessness.

But that's right where he wanted me—at the end of myself. I am like a toddler who will try and try to accomplish a task that is well beyond her physical or mental ability and wear herself out until finally crying out for help—generally in frustration. I think I can "be" or "do" my way into his good graces, but I will always come to the end of myself. Are you the toddler who tries too hard or the one who gives up before they even start? Both look a little silly. Especially when there is a loving and experienced mommy or daddy right beside them who delights in being helpful.

Our God is so merciful that he wants us at the end of ourselves so that we have no choice but to look to him. He wants us to come to him in our guilt when we have messed up yet again, or our shame that we haven't even tried today, or our pride that we tried and we got it right. Wherever you are today, and especially in the days to come, seek your wholeness in Jesus who did it all on our behalf, *perfectly,* and asks us to claim his standing before the Father.

1. Where are you on the spectrum of perfectionism? Trying too hard or too dejected to even try? Somewhere in between?

2. Why would God want us at the end of ourselves?

God, thank you for caring about me so much that you refuse to allow me to rely on myself. Teach me today a new way in which I can learn to rely on you. I want to be firm-footed in my trust in you so that no matter what may come, I know that I am yours.

Day 3:
No Accident

"And those who belong to Christ Jesus have crucified the flesh with its passions and desires. If we live by the Spirit, let us also keep in step with the Spirit."
Galatians 5: 24-25

In having a child, God has given us the perfect object lesson in coming to the end of ourselves. I don't find it coincidental that most of the people I know who struggle with perfectionism are women, and only women can physically bear a child. Just as God set plans for us in accordance with our gender roles, so also he sets specific challenges in our path for our sanctification from the tendencies of our flesh.

Perfectionism can look different for all of us. I had a friend in graduate school who couldn't sleep unless all of the dishes were washed or loaded into the dishwasher at night. Yet another friend won't leave the house unless she's in full makeup. Maybe these examples are neither here nor there to you, but what is your poison? Do you pride yourself on being in such lock-step with your husband that you can't imagine a day when your views on parenting might differ? Are you unable to leave work until your desk is clear and your to-do list void of unchecked boxes? Are you caught up on your Bible study/devotional plan/journaling goals and don't foresee a time when that might not be the case?

There's no way for you to be entirely prepared for the changes that come with motherhood. Personally, professionally, relationally, spiritually—the list goes on—you will simply never be the same. The changes were a gigantic, and very unexpected, shock to my system. I secretly thought that, sure, things would be different for a while. My body would get a little mushy and for a time I would get less sleep, but after a few months, it would all get back to normal. But that is not at all what God has called me to. The differences are radical. The changes were abrupt. The heartaches are more sharply painful and the joys are more inexpressible. I rely on God in ways I never did before.

His plans are best. His ways are all good. It is no accident that you are the woman in your relationship and that this joy/burden/duty/delight/source of sanctification falls to you and not to your husband. Ask the Lord to reveal to you what passions of the flesh may be small aches now, but could turn into gaping, festering wounds if not addressed before years of parenting are under your belt. Only the Great Physician is able to identify the problem and heal in his mighty power.

1. Can you identify a passion or desire of the flesh that drives you to perfectionism or achievement in a specific area? If not, spend some time in prayer asking the Lord to gently show you.

2. What would living by the Spirit and walking by the Spirit look like for you in this stage of life?

Lord God, as your child I want to hate what you hate and love what you love. Show me how to walk by your Spirit to battle untruth and goals or requirements that I or others put on myself. I want your opinion of me to be the only one I give importance to.

Day 4:
A Night Out

"For God alone, O my soul, wait in silence, for my hope is from him. He only is my rock and my salvation, my fortress; I shall not be shaken. On God rests my salvation and my glory; my mighty rock, my refuge is God. Trust in him at all times, O people; pour out your heart before him; God is a refuge for us."

Psalm 62: 5-8

You glance in the mirror at the deep-purple wrap dress and wonder at how it really doesn't look so bad. Combined with the eye makeup and the hair that seems almost relieved to be styled for the first time in two weeks, you think you really don't look quite so bad at all. Your husband yells from the kitchen that the babysitter is here, and you tell him you'll just pump real fast and be out in twenty minutes, ready to go. You hook yourself up to the monstrosity of the modern milk machine and pray that it will buy you at least three hours of pain-free, leak-free, uninterrupted date night. You finish in record time, slip into the black pumps with barely an audible squawk of pain, grab your tiny—not a diaper bag—clutch off the bed and open the door, ready for a real-life date.

Puke. He's cleaning puke off his pants. "I'm sure it was just too much on her tummy without a burp," he says nervously, glancing at the wide-eyed babysitter. The baby looks your way and starts to cry. You drop your clutch and go to reach for her out of the babysitter's hesitant grip, and just as you get her into your hands, it happens again. Thankfully not on your dress, but not so thankfully, on the carpet. The baby is now wailing, the babysitter looks like she is planning the quickest escape route, and you can't decide who you will join.

Ah, the joys of motherhood. But it's one thing to take the ups and downs yourself, and a whole different thing when they begin to affect the relationship you hold most dearly in all the world. Your body will be different, your conversations will be about poop, your free time will evaporate, your sex drive may seem like a mystical unicorn you once believed in, and it will really only be a matter of weeks before you wonder the same old thing that countless couples before you have wondered: "How did we ever think we were busy before?"

Where is God in all of this? How could this possibly be his plan when he says all his plans are *good?* Why do I feel so discontent when all I wanted for so long was a baby? Will my marriage ever go back to normal?

Wait in silence. Trust in Him. Pour out your heart before Him. He is a rock, refuge, salvation, and stronghold. He holds your salvation and your glory. God alone is your refuge.

1. Is your marriage in a good spot? Are there any conversations you need to have?

2. Would you commit to memorizing all or a portion (even a line) of this scripture? The Holy Spirit works with what we have committed to memory in our most difficult times.

Today I pray for my marriage and for the place we are in right now. Grant us the grace to roll with the punches and to laugh and love in deeper ways than we ever have before.

Day 5:
Not My Will

*"The Lord of hosts has sworn: 'As I have planned,
so it shall be, and as I have purposed, so shall it stand.'"*
Isaiah 14:24

If you're one for imagining, you've probably imagined your future family before. Let me guess, it's some variation of happy marriage; beautiful, obedient children; nice house—not too big but big enough; and just enough money for that week-long vacation once a year. When I look around I realize many others probably had much the same dream, and few of them are actually living it. I consider my friend with the wayward twenty-something year old son who considers himself agnostic; another with an autistic son; yet another whose family just received a terminal diagnosis for their infant daughter. I'm guessing none of them saw their futures just as they are. I see their realities, and I grieve. I would never consider that their reality may one day become mine. And if it were to, it would be just what the Lord had intended and planned for me. No mistakes, no accidents.

That is a very big and painful pill for me to swallow. I assent intellectually to the all-powerfulness of God, but I struggle to reconcile all the hurts of the world to his continued promises that he is good and holy and for me. I acknowledge that there is no evil in him, and yet bad things happen to "good people." But as RC Sproul most eloquently said when he struggled with a difficult theological topic, "Though it must be true and though I have to believe, preach, and teach it, I do not have to like it."[1]

Sometimes I just plain don't like it. Sometimes it doesn't make sense. Yet there is a stop in my logic, a place where I have no choice but to bow my knee before the Father and assent "not my will but yours." A place where I concede his God-ness and my, well, *not*. And I have no choice because of Christ and what he accomplished on the cross. What a beautiful lack of choice: "Lord, to whom shall we go? You have the words of eternal life." (John 6:68)

Where does this leave me when things don't turn out just as me, myself and *I intended* and just as me, myself and *I planned?* There is comfort in relinquishing all ultimate planning responsibility to a wise and kind-hearted Father. His plans will stand, no matter what. His intentions are for our ultimate good and his ultimate glory, no matter what. May my knee bow and my heart assent, for there is nowhere else to go. What he has in mind for my life might not look like my idea of a happy family, but it is sure to be the one guaranteed for the best good and glory—for both of us.

1. Name three expectations you have about the future of your family, generic or specific.

2. Ask the Father to give you the willingness to sacrifice those idols on the altar to him, should he require them.

Father, I repent of my expectations of this life. Only you are good, and only you are in charge. Please grant me the ability to bow my heart before you and to know that you have ordered and numbered my days just as you see fit.

Week Five

Comparison

Day 1:
Whom Am I Following?

*"Peter turned and saw the disciple whom Jesus loved
following them ... When Peter saw him,
he said to Jesus, 'Lord, what about this man?'
Jesus said to him, 'If it is my will that he remain until
I come, what is that to you? You follow me!'"*

John 21:20-22

Jesus is extending an invitation to us to follow him in the midst of a society prone to compare. Jesus' abrupt response invites us to pause and consider his tone, his heart, his longing for Peter, even his longing for you and for me.

For many of us, there exists an ideal of what a Christian wife and mother should look like and the results she should attain. Maybe this Christian wife and mother looks like the together and orderly Mary Poppins. Maybe she looks like the tenderhearted and innovative Mary Bailey in *It's a Wonderful Life*. Maybe she looks like the flexible and carefree Maria in *Sound of Music*. Or, maybe she is a family member, friend, or acquaintance. But as we consider this picture, we often consciously and subconsciously place our contentment in how well we are progressing towards being like her. Often, this is fleshed out with our children. We experience feelings of security or insecurity in how well we and our children are measuring up to this societal norm, ideal, or person. Like Peter, we turn our gaze away from the Lord, and ask, "What about this person?"

There is nothing wrong with practically considering what a Christian wife and mother looks like in flesh and blood. However, the moment we begin to measure our success through comparison is when we begin to follow another. "For am I now seeking the approval of man, or of God? Or am I trying to please man? If I were still trying to please man, I would not be a servant of Christ" (Gal. 1:10).

So what does it look like to hear Jesus' call to follow him? "God chose what is low and despised in the world, even things that are not, to bring to nothing things that are, so that no human being might boast in the presence of the God. He is the source of our life in Christ Jesus, whom God made our wisdom and our righteousness and sanctification and redemption. Therefore, as it is written, 'Let the one who boasts, boast in the Lord'" (1 Cor. 1:28-31). As we hear Jesus' tone, heart, and longing, our gaze turns towards him and turns away from others. We are reminded of the dependence his call requires. He equips us as mothers for precisely our children in exactly the way he wants us to parent. His humble life, sacrificial death, and glorious resurrection provide the framework for us to follow.

1. What ideals come to mind when I hear "Christian wife" and "Christian mother?" Describe them.

2. What resonates within me as I consider the words of Jesus, "You follow me?"

Father, I thank you that you are the source of my life in Christ Jesus. Give me fresh faith to follow you as I wade through the waters of being a Christ-following wife and mother.

Day 2:
Liberty From Measuring Up

> *"Therefore, since we have been justified by faith,*
> *we have peace with God through our Lord Jesus Christ.*
> *Through him we have also obtained access by faith*
> *into this grace in which we stand,*
> *and we rejoice in hope of the glory of God."*
> Romans 5:1-2

It was a risk. I took my toddler to the grocery store during lunchtime. I distracted him as he "drove" the racecar grocery cart through the produce section, and I hurried to find the remaining items needed. With his hunger and impatience escalating, I frantically approached checkout. The whining began. Seconds later, he was in the midst of a full-blown fit, refusing to sit in the racecar. As I struggled in vain to calm my screaming son and think of a creative solution for transferring the groceries onto the conveyor belt, a sales associate appeared and offered to unload my groceries. In the moment when all I could hear was my wailing child, all I could feel was my embarrassment, and all I could think was how I shouldn't be embarrassed of my son, the employee's gesture reminded me I was not alone. I encountered grace. She did for me what I was unable to do for myself.

The reality is we will never measure up to our own standards; to the assumed or true standards of others; or to the standards prescribed in the Bible. But God, in his loving kindness, often allows us to have exposing "grocery store moments" as we are confronted with our futile efforts. This is where grace steps in. This is where grace fills the gap.

We are at peace with God and have access to his presence and grace through Jesus. He is the only person who has ever measured up. He invites us to receive the grace he offers. He walks alongside us filling in the gaps. Because we are his daughters, his grace is freely given despite our best or most poorly executed efforts. In effect, we obtain "motherhood righteousness" through his perfect life. Before God, Christ's righteousness is imputed to us. It is as if we have mothered our children perfectly and loved them unconditionally. We no longer have to measure up. The measuring stick with our name on it came up short and was broken at the cross. Our standing is not dependent on how well we, or our babies, are doing relative to any of our standards. This is our hope and peace that fuels us to risk going to the grocery store again, to love our children despite their weaknesses, and to live comfortably in our own skin as mothers.

1. How have I experienced and responded to "grocery store moments" in my life?

2. If I no longer have to measure up, how might that impact the choices I make as a mother?

Abba Father, help me to live in the freedom of knowing that Christ has set me free so that I would not "submit again to a yoke of slavery" in my attempts to measure up. (Galatians 5:1 ESV)

Day 3:
Looking For Answers?

"For we are powerless against this great horde that is coming against us. We do not know what to do, but our eyes are on you."
2 Chronicles 20:12

In the passage above, King Jehoshaphat's prayer echoes the cry of many new (and seasoned) mothers' hearts. *What should I do?* This fundamental question has exponential variations when it comes to mothering. For instance, what should I do when: She's inconsolable; he isn't sleeping at night; she's not gaining weight; he's gaining too much; she isn't ready for kindergarten? And the list goes on and on.

In raising our children, we encounter numerous questions each day. Some questions have to be answered in a split second. Others can be contemplated for days, weeks, months, and years.

Regardless, answers must be found and decisions must be made. So where do we go for the answers?

Simply enter a Google search, and within seconds you will receive numerous answers to your questions. Often, the answers we seek and the answers we receive are methods or formulas that we are to apply for a desired result. However, underneath every *"What should I do?"* question lies the deeper questions: What can help me? Who is going to rescue me?

Grappling with these deeper questions is far more difficult than entering a Google search. Oftentimes, sitting before the Lord in the messiness of unanswered questions feels powerless and confusing. It is unsettling as we lift our eyes upward in prayer, like Jehoshaphat, because it feels risky. Will God answer? Will he show me what to do? Fortunately, we serve a loving Father who promises to "supply every need of [ours] according to his riches in glory in Christ Jesus" (Phil. 4:19). God's love and faithful promise to meet our needs is our comfort and strength in times of confusion and pain.

So, is there anything wrong with implementing a method? The answer is a resounding no. God promises to meet us in our weakness. In doing so, he frequently provides creative solutions. In his sovereign love and mercy, he may use books, blogs, advice from others, or even a Google search as a means to help us in our time of need. More importantly, he promises to meet us as we get still before Him. In stillness, we may discover the question is not "What should I do?" but "What is this situation exposing about my belief in God and/or what I believe about myself?"

1. When faced with the question *"What should I do?"* where do I consistently turn?

2. When faced with a friend or family member's question regarding a decision I have made, how do I consistently respond?

Father, increase my belief that I am not alone in the battles I face each day. May I respond to your invitation "and see the salvation of the Lord on [my] behalf" (2 Chron. 20:17).

Day 4:
New Mercies

"Remember not the former things, nor consider the things of old. Behold, I am doing a new thing; now it springs forth, do you not perceive it? I will make a way in the wilderness and rivers in the desert."
Isaiah 43:18-19

Do I have what it takes? This question has haunted me throughout my life driving much of my thoughts and behavior.

In an attempt to answer the question, I have surrounded myself with women similar to me thinking: "if these women have what it takes, then I must have what it takes." I have also subtly manipulated conversation to hear others tell me I am a good mother or that "yes" I do have what it takes. Yet any assurance I received was short-lived, and it wasn't long before I needed the next one. Each approach has led me to either pride and overconfidence or disappointment and emptiness.

The truth is most of us ask similar questions. The problem is to whom are we asking. Asking ourselves or asking others will either leave us empty or overconfident. Only our

Creator is equipped to answer the questions deep within our souls. He is the one who knew us before the foundation of the world, formed each of us in our mother's womb, saw fit to give us each the gift of a child and the role of a mother. As our loving Father, God longs for us to run to him with our questions, our struggles, and our successes. He longs to lovingly whisper to us that he has given us a new heart and placed his spirit within us. We are now able to respond in faith to his leading. He is the one making all things new. He is the one who provides new mercies each morning. He is the one inviting us to remember not the former things but to look in faith to him as he molds each of us into the mother he created us to be. We are made in the image of God. Just as no two children are alike, each mother is unique and offers her uniqueness to her children in a way that reflects God as no one else can.

Because of the finished work of Christ, the pressure is off. The extremes of feeling insecure or overconfident are no longer where we have to go when we wonder how we are doing as a mother. Everything changes. God looks at us as his children and sees Jesus' perfect life. We have his favor as his daughters. And just as we experience feelings of pride and joy as we watch our children develop into who they are created to be, God looks on our efforts in faith, the effective and ineffective ones, and is pleased. The truth is, in Christ, we do have what it takes.

1. How has God uniquely shaped me to be a mother? Be specific.

2. What "new thing" is God showing me as I read this reflection? What am I prompted to believe?

"I praise you, for I am fearfully and wonderfully made" (Psalm 139:14 ESV). Help me to hear your voice and take my questions to you. Help me to believe you have equipped me to parent my child.

Day 5:
Living in the Gray

"'Judge not, that you be not judged. For with the judgment you pronounce you will be judged, and with the measure you use it will be measured to you. Why do you see the speck that is in your brother's eye, but do not notice the log that is in your own eye? Or how can you say to your brother, 'Let me take the speck out of your eye,' when there is a log in your own eye? You hypocrite, first take the log out of your own eye, and then you will see clearly to take the speck out of your brother's eye.'"

Matthew 7:1-5

In this familiar passage, Jesus prohibits one kind of judging but approves another. He points out that condemning others for their faults is a failure to extend forgiveness and thus a failure to love. On the other hand, a gentle and humble correction that first recognizes one's own faults is the most loving thing a person can do for a brother or sister caught in sin.

As new mothers, some of us are prone towards judging others. We have our methods and formulas and experience pride when they work. This leads us to look down on those whose methods are different. A dear friend once told me that every new mother needs "new mom grace." Extending grace may simply be providing a safe place for another mother to try and perhaps fail without passing judgment, providing solutions or correction. Scripture does not provide a magic formula that can be applied by all mothers in all situations. This piece of wisdom did not resonate within my heart until I began sailing through the uncharted waters of pregnancy and having a newborn. It was here I discovered a growing desire for grace and mercy from the Lord and from others.

Many times we operate as though everything is black and white and every situation has a magic formula. This leads us to the type of judging condemned by Christ. However, all areas of life are not black and white. Raising a child seems the grayest of grays. This is humbling, sobering, and scary. Yet living in the gray can be a place of freedom and hope as we look to the Lord to lead us by his Spirit. Thankfully, we have a high priest who is able to sympathize with us in our every weakness: "Let us then with confidence draw near to the throne of grace, that we may receive mercy and find grace to help in time of need" (Heb. 4:16). As we receive grace and mercy, we are enabled to extend it.

However, we are never called to demand grace from anyone, even when we do not experience "mom grace" from others. Instead, we are called to extend it. In such times, we draw comfort in the fact that God's grace is sufficient.

1. When have you experienced others judging you for not making a particular decision? When have you judged others?

2. What might extending and receiving "mom grace" look like for you right now?

Lord, grant me repentance that I may be quick to see where I have judged. Help me to humbly look to you for sufficient grace when I experience judgment from family members.

Week Six

Loneliness

Day 1:
So Alone

> *"He was despised and rejected by men; a man of sorrows,*
> *and acquainted with grief; and as one from whom men*
> *hide their faces he was despised, and we esteemed him not.*
> *Surely he has borne our griefs and carried our sorrows;*
> *yet we esteemed him stricken, smitten by God, and afflicted."*
> Isaiah 53:3-4

I don't remember a time in my life when I didn't long to be a mother. So you can imagine that the moment I found out I was expecting brought me nothing but pure joy. The months could not go by fast enough for me to hold and meet my sweet baby. However, things didn't go exactly as I planned when I brought my "sweet baby" home. I'm pretty sure I cried the entire first night he was home, saying things like: "He won't sleep unless I hold him," "He's not getting enough to eat," "I'm so tired, I don't know what to do," and the best line of the night was when I looked at my husband and said, "Let's move to Mexico, my mom will take care of him. She loves babies."

Eight weeks later, I was still crying at the drop of a hat and wondering if I would ever be back to my old self again. At my post partum check up, I explained to my doctor what had been going on, and that's when she said, "You are suffering from post partum depression."

I felt so alone. I watched my friends have babies, and

they were so in love. Why was I going through this? This was supposed to be the happiest time of my life. Then, God gently reminded me of how alone Jesus must have felt when he was the only perfect person living in a world full of sin. Even members of his own family didn't understand who he was, and "not even his brothers believed in him" (John 7:5). They were sinners; he was not. The end of his life must have been the loneliest. He hung from a cross bearing our sins and was forsaken by his own Father. More than any person, Jesus understands our loneliness, sorrows, grief, and confusion, but he doesn't leave us there! Acts 15:8 says that God knows our hearts and has given us the Holy Spirit as a comfort and counselor. From the beginning, one of Scripture's refrains is *God is with you.* He entered the darkness at the beginning of the world, he entered the darkness of our sin, he walks with us through streams of righteousness and waves that seem to overcome us. God even called his Son Immanuel—God with us—as a way to remind us that he will never (never!) leave us. Take heart! You are known. You are understood. You are His.

1. When you feel lonely what do you run to for comfort? Think and meditate on scripture that will allow you to run to God and not the world for satisfaction.

2. Think of a time of loneliness in your life. Did you feel the presence of God? If so, how?

Dear Jesus, thank you for reminding us that you are always with us. Draw near to us and help us to constantly long for you. May you go before us as we raise your children that you have so graciously given to us for this short time. Thank you for understanding our loneliness and constantly meeting us where we are.

Day 2:
Isolation for the Stay-at-Home-Mom

"And these words which I command you today shall be in your heart. You shall teach them diligently to your children, and shall talk of them when you sit in your house, when you walk by the way, when you lie down, and when you rise."

Deuteronomy 6:6-7

While I was single, I worked for a nonprofit organization that ran mostly off volunteer work. Most of the women who volunteered were stay-at-home moms or had been stay-at-home moms when their children were young. I remember thinking what wonderful lives they had. How it must be so nice to not have to work and spend all day with your children while your husband provides for you. Fast forward a few years later to me being married and a stay-at-home mom, and I can't help but laugh at what I thought was an easy job. I had more than glamorized it. What I didn't realize: how much work it is, how set apart from the world you feel, how guilty you feel most days because you don't know if you're doing a good job, how you're constantly praying that the fruit of your labor pays off, and how hard it is to appreciate your children when you are with them twenty-four hours a day, seven days a week. And then there's the guilt you feel when there is one income— "He makes it; I spend it." So much guilt, uncertainty, and really hard (and wonderful) days.

The beautiful mothers who have gone before us always say, "Soak up every minute because it goes by fast." They're wise women and I like to grab hold of what they tell me, but when my child is screaming through the grocery store, I also kind of want to punch them. Whether I'm soaking up the moments or ready for them to pass, the real longing of our hearts is that one day we'll be looking at a once-child that has grown into a man or woman who longs for Jesus, who walks with him and knows his love. On the hard (and easy) days, I remember that this is a season that we have been called to and that God has hand-picked each moment of the days we have with our little ones, so that, like the old hymn says, we will see him more clearly, love him more dearly, and follow him more nearly.

Deuteronomy 6 talks about the words of God that are on our hearts—namely, to love him with all our heart, soul, and might (v. 5). Before we ever teach his love to our children, God desires for us to know his love personally. So today, rest in and reflect on the love God has for you. You are his chosen one, his beloved, his delight, and his joy, regardless of how you feel or act. You are His.

1. What have you learned about yourself since being a (stay-at-home) mom? What have you learned about God?

2. How have you experienced God's love for you this week?

Thank you Jesus for our sweet babies. Go before us as we take on such a big job. Help us to be content and to persevere when we are tired and weary. Thank you for being our heavenly father and loving us.

Day 3:
Isolation for the Working Mom

"Praise the LORD! Blessed is the man who fears the LORD, who greatly delights in his commandments! His offspring will be mighty in the land; the generation of the upright will be blessed."
Psalm 112:1-2

If you're a working mom, you've probably thought something along these lines:
- "Will my child grow up to resent me for not staying at home?"
- "I was scared that she wouldn't remember me because she would be spending more time with people other than me."
- "How will I do two jobs well? (working and being a mom)
- "I won't be as good of a mom if I work."
- "People will think I'm not as godly because I work outside the home."

Whether your maternity leave is just now ending and you're mentally preparing to put your child in someone else's care for the first time, or if you've been back at work for a while, you know the difficulty of being away from your child and entrusting him or her to someone else. Try as you might, all the preparation in the world won't make that first day back easy. You'll spend the majority of the first day back to work wondering if your baby is safe and what they're doing every second of the day. And even if you've been a working mom for a while, you still wonder how your child is doing throughout the day. Guilt may set in, and you may start to think about the luxury of being an at-home mom. You might think how much better they have it because they get to spend every day with their babies, which could cause you to resent your job and your co-workers because, in your mind, no one understands how you feel.

Some women love their career and feel called to work outside the home, while others need to help in providing for their families. There isn't any scripture that shows favor toward the working mom or the at-home mom, but it does teach that our first and highest calling is not as a mother but as a child of God--to know and love him. Whether we are working in the home or outside of the home, we are called to be women who fear the Lord and delight in his Word. Our worth and our children's salvation don't depend on whether we choose to stay at home or work outside the home. Jesus alone does the heart work in all of us. Let's be diligent to pray for the hearts of our children, because whether they are with us or whether we are apart, all their moments (and ours!) are His.

1. What are your biggest fears about trusting your child in the care of another? What does God say about fear?

2. How can we pray for our children more diligently?

Thank you, Lord, for loving us through our fears and insecurities. Thank you for reminding us that you are for our children and us. Thank you that we are your children and you have adopted us into your glorious kingdom. May we never stray from your truth.

Day 4:
Illness

*"The heart of a man plans his way,
but the Lord establishes his steps."*
Proverbs 16:9

It was the morning of December 21; our bags were packed and ready to go see family for Christmas. We knew that our two-year-old son had been fussy all morning, but we just thought, "It's just one of *those* mornings." My husband picked him up and sat down on the couch with him to comfort him, and he went right to sleep. Let's just say, that never happens! I felt his head, and as his temperature rose, my heart sank. I felt terrible for him and at the same time I knew we were going to have to tell my parents we couldn't come see them for Christmas. We took him straight to the doctor to find out he had the flu. His doctor said that it would probably be a solid week before he was better. So, the next phone call was made to my husband's family to tell them we couldn't do Christmas with them either. This was the first year in my entire life that I did not see my family (or any family for that matter) for Christmas, and while it may sound a little dramatic, we were heartbroken. How could we not see a single person for Christmas?

There are so many times in our lives when our plans are going to fail, especially when children are involved. The Lord is constantly reminding us to keep our eyes on him and to remember that his ways are better. It's not that our desires for time with family or healthy children are bad; they're actually good! But if they're all we desire, then they're shortsighted because they desire a gift over the giver, and what we can see over what we can't see.

I recently read a quote by Sally Clarkson that said "God is parenting us while we are parenting our children." Isn't that so true? I think about how I long for my son to truly understand who God is. And to think that the Father longs for our hearts far more than I long for my son's heart to belong to God! I simply cannot wrap my brain around that. It's at times when our plans are altered and we feel isolated and set apart from the world that we can stop and remember that our heavenly father is pursuing us and is with us.

1. Think of a time when your plans did not go as expected. What did you learn from it?

2. Think about the Lord's pursuit for you. What has the Lord done in and through you since you became a Christian?

Lord, thank you that your ways are better than our ways. Thank you for loving us when we are unlovable and for pursuing us through our sin. Even in the loneliest moments of our lives, keep our hearts fixed on you.

Day 5:
Community

"Now may our God and Father himself, and our Lord Jesus Christ, direct our way to you, and may the Lord make you increase and abound in love to one another and for all, as we do for you, so that he may establish your hearts blameless in holiness before our God and Father at the coming of our Lord Jesus Christ with all His saints."

1 Thessalonians 3:11-13

Living in the South among Christian friends and family can cause us to take for granted the beautiful community that we have. It's easy for us to get caught up in the busyness of our own lives and forget that living in community is not just a gift (Jeremiah 31:33) but also a command: "And let us consider how to stir up one another to love and good works, not neglecting to meet together, as is the habit of some, but encouraging one another, and all the more as you see the Day drawing near" (Heb. 10:24-25).

As moms of young children, we're limited a lot in what we can do, especially when our children are in the infant/toddler stage. (Let's be honest: it takes twice as long just to get out of the house!) It's easy for our worlds to become small. On the one hand, having kids does shrink our worlds (sometimes in wonderful, restful ways), but on the other, having kids can become an excuse not to be a part of something bigger than ourselves, namely the Church and the fellowship of believers. In his mercy, God gave us other believers to share this journey through life. When Paul was in prison, he wrote letters to encourage the church. He knew about the need to continue to spread God's word and love one another no matter the circumstance (Eph. 3:20-21). Being a part of a community is both outward (service) and inward (being served). It's a place to encourage others, but also a place to receive support and words of truth for yourself.

As mothers, we're regularly living in some sort of guilt

and are full of questions; what a gift to have other women who are in the same boat walking alongside us, helping us with our questions and children, and pointing us toward Jesus. The point goes beyond just a plea to "get involved," although you may find that life-giving. I'm encouraging you to be a part of the body of believers in whatever way God has called you so that you experience the unique gifts God gives when we're a part of a community of believers—encouragement, faith, purity, and joy.

1. Think of reasons that you may run from the church. What lies do you believe?

2. Do you have a Christian community that you are involved in? If so, what have you learned while having these people in your life?

Thank you, Lord, for community and others who love you and your word. Please help us to not take these people for granted to and love one another as you love the church. Thank you for showing us our need for relationships. Grow us in more understanding of the church. Amen.

Week Seven
Expecting Emotions

Day 1:
In the Image of God

"How long, O LORD? Will you be angry forever?
Will your jealousy burn like fire?"
Psalm 79:5

"For God so loved the world..."
John 3:16a

"Reproaches have broken my heart, so that I am in despair."
Psalm 69:20

"And taking with him Peter and the two sons of Zebedee,
he began to be sorrowful and troubled."
Matthew 26:37

"Peace I leave with you; my peace I give to you ...
Let not your hearts be troubled, neither let them be afraid."
John 14:27

From Genesis to Revelation, the Bible is filled with emotion—God's and man's. Both scripture and our personal experience testify that both God and man are emotional beings. But God made us in his image and in his likeness; why wouldn't we be emotional creatures? Our emotions are tools in his hands. God created them; they are good and useful.

When expecting, I thought my baby would burp rainbows and that all would be perfect, but it just wasn't so. Personally, I experienced a wide range of emotions, and if you've given birth or adopted, your emotions may be set on fire too.

Everyone wants to experience positive emotions, but the negative ones can be useful if we have eyes to see them for what they are—an opportunity for us to be led to Christ. They help us form conclusions about our own hearts and spot idolatry. They call us to repentance and hope. Emotions can also teach us to be thankful for God's mercy and love – not to mention his power at work within us.

It's easy to see negative emotions like fear, anger, sorrow, or pride as problems and to see positive emotions like gratitude, joy, hope, and confidence in Christ as solutions. But the truth is that God created and experienced both negative and positive emotions to help us know Him more fully. Jesus grieved over the loss of a friend, got angry with the Pharisees in the temple, and begged God to make a way for his children other than the cross. But he also thanked God regularly, called his disciples to hope in something bigger than this world, and rejoiced over even one sinner repenting. If we are made in his image, our emotional range will mimic His. The question is: how do we allow God to rule our emotions rather than our emotions to rule us? Clearly, the answer isn't to eliminate all negative emotions. A good place to start might be to ask: "What are you up to here, God? Where are you in this?" And then listen, expectantly waiting and watching for him to reveal his way—even when his way is through a valley.

1. What are some positive emotions you experience? What negative emotions do you struggle with the most?

2. Since God is an emotional being, what emotion do you appreciate the most about him? Pause and give thanks for it.

Father, I have a love/hate relationship with my emotions. Bring them under the control of your Holy Spirit by your grace. Thank you for being the Hope of Salvation (Psalm 65:5).

Day 2:
Gratitude vs. Anger

"Through him then let us continually offer up a sacrifice of praise to God, that is, the fruit of lips that acknowledge his name."
Hebrews 13:15

"... Be filled with the Spirit, addressing one another in psalms and hymns and spiritual songs, singing and making melody to the Lord with your heart, giving thanks always and for everything to God the Father in the name of our Lord Jesus Christ."
Ephesians 5:18-20

I realized how gratitude changes a heart years ago when I was struggling with my husband's habit of leaving clothing lying about: pants on the floor, socks flung on a chair. I mentally complained – watching anger rise as I stirred the pot of resentment. I obsessed on the "socks and pants" and couldn't release the anger. One day I tried a new approach. As I picked up clothing, I gave thanks for my husband and his good qualities. I found my heart changing toward him. Anger became gratitude, and when he walked in the door, I was a kinder woman.

The same thing happens to my heart when I'm angry or disappointed with God about my life and circumstances. Hebrews 13:15 says, "Through him then let us continually offer up a sacrifice of praise to God." Sometimes I have to force the words of gratitude as a sacrifice, like when my washer breaks or my boss doesn't see how hard I've worked—my children whine incessantly, or when international disaster breaks out. But thankfully my heart often follows the words. Praise can bring perspective to angry hearts: *Thank you for washing machines at all, for the gift of a job and an income, for children who are alive and healthy, for a country where I can freely worship.* It's not a fix for hard circumstances, but a new lens through which to see them.

Praise diffuses the anger we feel when our perceived rights are violated. Praise releases our rights into the hands of a sovereign and loving God. It helps change our perspective so that we can see his love in the midst of disappointment (not getting sleep or being able to have a meal in peace). Gratitude is not a magic pill, but it is a strategy for redirecting our hearts toward the truth of God's unfailing love and faithfulness.

If you are naturally grateful, keep it up, but if you struggle as I do, practice. It might feel hypocritical when you begin, but Psalm 50:23 says, "The one who offers thanksgiving as his sacrifice glorifies me; to one who orders his way rightly I will show the salvation of God!"

1. After you become a mother, what are some things you might be angry about? What might you be thankful for instead?

2. Gratitude and praise sometimes feel like sacrifices, especially when we want what we don't have. Can you imagine why God might use these as instruments for his purposes?

Dear Father, please open my eyes to see your grace and mercy in my life. I am often blinded by my resentment over things that aren't as I imagined they would be. Life is often harder than I planned. Forgive my angry, complaining heart, and replace it with a heart of gratitude.

Day 3:
Hope vs. Fear

"My soul is bereft of peace; I have forgotten what happiness is; so I say, 'My endurance has perished; so has my hope from the Lord.' Remember my affliction and my wanderings, the wormwood and the gall! My soul continually remembers it and is bowed down within me. But this I call to mind, and therefore I have hope: The steadfast love of the Lord never ceases; his mercies never come to an end; they are new every morning; great is your faithfulness. 'The Lord is my portion,' says my soul, 'therefore I will hope in him.'"
Lamentations 3:17-24

Years ago, I was hammered by a situation I had never imagined possible. It involved a serious illness, and I could only envision the very worst that might happen later. A friend who listened as I sobbed on the other end of the telephone gave me great counsel that continues to help me. She said, "You are imagining a future where God doesn't exist." And that's exactly what I was doing. I jumped from my reality and allowed fear to paint a picture of the worst possible scenario for the future—a future where God would not be faithful or present.

In the above verses, the author suffers because Israel suffers. The prophet understands that Israel is going to be judged. His fears are going to be realized. But even then, his expressions of hope show that he understands that God is going to be present in the future: "The steadfast love of the Lord never ceases; his mercies are new every morning ... *'the Lord is my portion,'* says my soul, *'therefore I will hope in him'*" (Lam. 3:22-24).

When I was a young mom staying home with my children, I couldn't imagine a tomorrow that wasn't filled with loneliness, fatigue, or a frustrated need for deep spiritual friendships. I feared eternal unmet needs. I feared friendlessness and soullessness. I was afraid of being a woman bored to tears married to a husband I never saw. Not only was God faithful in the trenches of young motherhood to be present in both joyous and difficult moments, but he was also faithful in the future I couldn't see. Now, I have rich friendships and a deep, grace-filled soul thanks to Christ's faithfulness. I am not bored, and I see my husband often. I have a future I never imagined: some of it is better, some of it worse. My fears have not been realized, but new ones press their noses against the window wanting to get in. But no matter what happens, "The Lord is my portion" (my part, my sufficiency), "and therefore I will hope in him."

1. Think of your greatest fear about the future and use your concordance to find a scripture to address it. Encourage yourself to hope in the Lord.

2. None of us know the future, and we are foolish if we think we can. Think of a time in the past when you let your imagination run away with you, and when the time arrived, nothing was like what your imagined.

Father God, I don't want to live in fear. I want to be full of hope and faith. Please help me remember that you're faithful every day of my life, even if I don't see your fingerprints. Let me live in hope of your steadfast love and mercies that are new every morning.

Day 4
Joy vs. Sorrow

*"The Spirit of the Lord God is upon me,
because the Lord has anointed me to bring good news
to the poor; he has sent me to bind up the brokenhearted,
to proclaim liberty to the captives,
and the opening of the prison to those who are bound;
to proclaim the year of the Lord's favor,
and the day of vengeance of our God;
to comfort all who mourn; to grant to
those who mourn in Zion—to give them a
beautiful headdress instead of ashes,
the oil of gladness instead of mourning,
the garment of praise instead of a faint spirit..."*
Isaiah 61:1-3.

Isaiah 61 reminds us of the reasons Christ came. He didn't come because things are great, but because they are radically ruined. He came to the brokenhearted, the bound, the mourning, and the weak. He came bringing good news to our fallen condition: there is hope, and it is found in Christ.

When we're expecting or have young children, we can be a bit unstable emotionally. We alternate between ecstatic joy and oppressive fear many times a day. But crossing bridges prematurely is unbiblical, and as we saw earlier, we need to trust in the promise that God will be present in the future. He will help us handle whatever his sovereign grace has appointed to our lives. If there is grief or sorrow, he will bring comfort. "Therefore do not be anxious about tomorrow, for tomorrow will be anxious for itself. Sufficient for the day is its own trouble," Jesus teaches in Matthew 6:34. However, sorrow will come, and when it does, how are you going to fight for joy while you grieve?

John Piper says "All strategies in the fight for joy are directly or indirectly strategies to see Christ more fully."[2] So, how are you going to fight to see Christ more fully?

Biblical joy seeks its highest satisfaction in Christ and all that he is and has done for us. When we take time to consider the mercies in our lives, we might find joy rising from the ruins of our sorrowful hearts. Cultivating joy won't prevent or eliminate the cut of sorrow or grief, but fighting for it might keep us from hemorrhaging when events cut us deeply.

1. Below are some qualities of Christ that you can use as weapons in a fight for joy. Look up a few of the references and meditate on them. *Merciful* (Ps. 145:8); *Present* (Ps. 46:1-3); *Comforting* (II Cor. 3:1-5); *Strong* (Ps. 84: 5-7) *Father* (Gal. 4:4-7); *Righteous* (Phil. 3:8-10); *Hope-giver* (Heb. 10:19-23)

2. You might be experiencing joy right now without fighting for it. If so, take time to give thanks to God for all of his mercies and grace.

Teach me how to fight for joy, Lord. Open my eyes to see Christ more fully. Forgive me when I give more credit to evil than your power to redeem, sustain, and restore. Build up my faith. You are good, and I will trust in you!

Day 5:
How do I get there?
Confidence in Christ

"Let the one who boasts, boast in the Lord. For it is not the one who commends himself who is approved, but the one whom the Lord commends."

2 Corinthians 10:17-18

In our minds, we have certain laws about how we should live. Typically, when we're living by these laws we feel good about ourselves (pride); when we aren't, we face shame, guilt and remorse.

Most of my life, the word I heard most often in my head was, "Failure!" When I struggled to breast-feed and couldn't, when my baby cried for two or three hours, when the house was a wreck when my husband walked through the door, or when I didn't want my husband to touch me at the end of an exhausting day, I would hear the word, "Failure!" And that accusation never brought change or encouragement; rather, it pushed me further toward defeat. However, Christ brings an alternative to this kind of toxic self-evaluation.

Christian examination is a fine line to walk. It includes

seeing our sin and being repentant, but it also includes seeing Christ and being confident of his forgiveness and power to change us. One of the enemy's powerful tools is to neutralize our impact on the world through pride over our achievements, shame over our failures, guilt over our sins, and remorse over the things we have left undone. If we evaluate our lives through the lens of our own laws and ability, we will be undone, ineffective, and finding ourselves avoiding people and God. Or we might minimize our shortcomings and become prideful and independently self-confident rather than dependent on the power of Christ.

However, if we appraise ourselves with our eyes on the cross and the grace of God, both pride and shame fall away, and we can be encouraged that Christ is at work in us and will complete what he has begun in us. When we fail to meet our own expectations as a parent or wife, we can encourage ourselves with truth: "Not that we are sufficient in ourselves to claim anything as coming from ourselves, but our sufficiency is from God" (2 Cor. 3:5).

You have been gloriously created in the image of God, and he has supplied a source for your ongoing growth and transformation: Christ in you. It is the cross being applied to your sin. It is grace—always his all-sufficient grace for every moment of every day for the rest of your life.

1. Do you tend toward pride and self-confidence, or shame and helplessness? Does this attitude create a judgmental spirit, withdrawal, further determination, or deep condemnation? (Underline what applies.)

2. God desires our confidence to be in Him. With your tendencies, what might God want you to remember about his grace toward you? (Sufficiency? Wisdom? Presence in you? Forgiveness? Other?)

Thank you for living in me and helping me overcome pride and self-abasement. Thank you for allowing Christ to come so that I might have confidence in him and not in my own self.

Week Eight

Spiritual Life After Baby Arrives

Day 1:
Help Me to Never Forget!

*"Sing for joy, O heavens, and exult, O earth; break forth,
O mountains, into singing! For the Lord has comforted his people
and will have compassion on his afflicted. But Zion said,
'The Lord has forsaken me; my Lord has forgotten me.' '
Can a woman forget her nursing child,
that she should have no compassion on the son of her womb?
Even these may forget, yet I will not forget you.'"*

Isaiah 49:13-15

As I thought about the topic, "Spiritual Life after Baby Arrives," I was struck by a simple truth that pervades all of scripture: *God loves us passionately.* However, in the whirl of diapers, carpool, work, dinner, relationships—you name it!—that truth is so easily lost. You might, in the hormonal, sleep-deprived madness, forget God or feel like he has forgotten you. But still: he will remember you.

In Luke 12:6-7 we read, "Are not five sparrows sold for two pennies? And not one of them is forgotten before God. Why, even the hairs of your head are all numbered. Fear not; you are of more value than many sparrows." We matter to God, and if he is my Abba Father, I want him to matter to me, too. But I often get so caught up in the daily concerns of figuring out which fire to fight first that I forget both. Dishes screaming in the sink silence the whisper of God, the one that I really long to hear: "Come to me all you who labor and are heavy laden, and I will give you rest" (Matt. 11:28).

The scriptural encouragement to spend time with Jesus is God wooing us to himself. It's his attempt to suspend the harsh shouts of the world so we can ponder his preciousness and ours. It is a place to remember that he remembers us! His assurances don't adhere easily, so we must ask for help at remembering.

But how? you might be asking. Just give me the ten steps to being a godly mother; at least I can try to do them! Here comes performance. God doesn't give us a recipe; he gives us Himself. "Come," he says. That's it. "Come, and I will give you rest." He loves you and wants you just as you are—milk-stained, frustrated, un-showered as you may be. You are of great, unspeakable value to him!

1. What is your opinion of quiet times with God? Is it a checklist? A place of love? What old attitudes about "quiet times" are at odds with the idea that Christ is inviting you to remember his goodness?

2. How does the thought of God writing your name on his hand impact your heart? Use your imagination and see your name written there—right within the scars on Jesus' hands.

Thank you that you never forget me and that you have engraved me on your hand. Though I may forget you in my busyness or weariness, you won't ever forget me. In the weeks to come, please help me remember all these truths. Help me see that you do carry me and keep me – even when I forget.

Day 2:
One Thing Necessary

> *'Now as they went on their way, Jesus entered a village. And a woman named Martha welcomed him into her house. And she had a sister called Mary, who sat at the Lord's feet and listened to his teaching. But Martha was distracted with much serving. And she went up to him and said, 'Lord, do you not care that my sister has left me to serve alone? Tell her then to help me.' But the Lord answered her, 'Martha, Martha, you are anxious and troubled about many things, but one thing is necessary. Mary has chosen the good portion, which will not be taken away from her.'"*
>
> Luke 10:38-42

When a child enters our life, the demands of motherhood take priority, time evaporates, and we quickly find that old devotional patterns no longer work. But we know that we need to keep our hearts centered in Christ so we can have an eternal perspective and avoid toxic thoughts.

So, what is a new mom to do? How can you spend regular time with God without adding legalistic solutions or imperatives to your schedule rather than means of grace? How can I encourage a young mom in a time of life where hardly a minute seems her own? But I'd be remiss not to address the scriptural call of regular time with Jesus. This is tough. We would be served well to look for the middle ground of grace. Can I encourage you to be intentional but flexible with your time with God each day during this season? Can I encourage you to know yourself and your response to pressure situations—do you tend to be a Martha or a Mary?

Consider the word abide as you seek to figure a way into time with the Lord in this time of life. How can you continue in a state or place of abiding in Christ when your quiet times don't look like what they've previously been? He will meet you—he promises he will, and this season is from Him. You might spend one uninterrupted minute with God one day and fifteen the next . . . grace upon grace . . . think of him as a lover wooing you into stolen moments. Take the moments as they come—they're all leading you to draw constant life from Him.

Whether you tend to be more flexible or intentional, Jesus is after your heart, and you become like those you're around. So seek to be around Jesus. He's in all our moments. Pray for eyes to see him and a heart that will choose the one thing necessary when a thousand other things tug at your time.

1. Do you tend to be a Martha or a Mary?

2. What might be the motivation of Jesus' words to Martha? Condemnation? Hope? Love? Longing for more for Martha? What is he after?

Lord, help me to not be worried and upset about many things and to remember that only a few are needed. Remind me throughout the day to set aside my Martha-madness and choose a Mary-mind – that which is better and can't be taken from me.

Day 3:
Eyes Wide Open

"... Save your servant, who trusts in you—you are my God.
Be gracious to me, O Lord, for to you do I cry all the day.
Gladden the soul of your servant, for to you, O Lord,
do I lift up my soul. For you, O Lord, are good and forgiving,
abounding in steadfast love to all who call upon you.
Give ear, O Lord, to my prayer . . . In the day
of my trouble I call upon you, for you answer me . . .
For you are great and do wondrous things; you alone are God."

Psalm 86:2-7, 10

Many years ago, the Lord began to teach me to pray. I wanted to become a woman of prayer and began to learn by praying with other young mothers. We prayed while sitting on the floor with our children crawling on us and beside us and with our eyes wide open. How else is a young mom supposed to pray?

At first my prayers were lopsided; they were deep pleadings with many tears and excessive repentance. After praying I often walked away disheartened. God graciously began to teach me to envelop my prayers with praise and with promises from his Word. As I learned to pray that way, my eyes became wide open to the glory, lovingkindness, and faithfulness of the Lord. As he became more beautifully defined in my heart by my praise and worship, despair shrank, hope was kindled, and the reward of my prayers wasn't limited to a specific answer (although he often graciously gave that); it was knowing Him. He became the object and goal. God wants us to pray with our eyes wide open—open to his glory, open to the world around us, and open to him as we go about our daily business.

I find that if I'm not intentional about worshipping while praying, I simply worry and complain in front of God and end up bitter or sad at the end of the day. With this intentionality, the prayer, "I'm overwhelmed and very lonely today" becomes, "I'm overwhelmed and very lonely today, but you promised to strengthen me and help me (Job 4:3); you said you will never leave me or forsake me (Deut. 31:8). Thank you for your faithfulness to me, O God, even if I don't feel it right now." Having eyes wide open to the glory of God while praying restores hope. Wrapping prayers in praise is a biblical model. Moses and David did it; Jesus and Paul did it; so should we.

1. When going through your day, are your eyes wide open to the words you are speaking to yourself? To God? How are the words impacting your heart?

2. In the Scripture above, David practices praise within a cry for help. When praying, what are some character qualities or promises of God that bring you comfort in your current situation?

Dear Father, remind me to give thanks for your blessings and mercies. Help me remember that there is no particular way or time to pray, and I can pray while doing dishes or feeding my child. Help me to keep my eyes wide open to the needs around me and to your eternal glory and majesty.

Day 4:
All of Life

"Shout for joy to God, all the earth; sing the glory of his name;
give to him glorious praise! Say to God,
'How awesome are your deeds! So great is your power
that your enemies come cringing to you.
All the earth worships you and sings praises to you;
they sing praises to your name.' Selah
Come and see what God has done:
he is awesome in his deeds toward the children of man."

Psalm 66:1-5

I love being led to think about God's worth on Sunday mornings. My initial training on how to worship took place in the sanctuary, and my worship is renewed there weekly. However, I've discovered that worship is more than singing a song or listening to a sermon. True worship engages my heart in a process of thanksgiving, admiration, adoration, and action. The kind of worship God loves also must be done in spirit and truth (John 4:22), and can be done anywhere at anytime by his grace.

Quite frankly, my sweetest moments of worship have taken place in solitude or in sudden moments of insight during a normal day. In worship, I see God in the light of his word and lift my voice and bend my heart before him. That is worship.

Becoming a mother gives you the opportunity to see God with new eyes. You might begin to understand God's love for you more clearly. Your child's utter dependence can remind you of your dependence on the Father. Your faithfulness to meet your child's needs can reveal God's faithfulness to you. Your child's screams for instant comfort might convict you of your bratty insistence for ease, and through your impatience, God can reveal his eternal patience. Take these simple, daily insights as opportunities to worship. They are gifts to you.

While comparing Old and New Covenant worship, John

Piper says, "The whole thrust (of worship) is being taken off of ceremony and seasons and places and forms and is being shifted to what is happening in the heart—not just on Sunday but every day and all the time *in all of life*" [3] (emphasis mine). Worship in community when you can, but worship in all of life.

1. How would you define worship, and how does worship impact you?

2. Imagine yourself as a baby looking into the face of her mother. When I nursed my children, they would touch my face, smile, or have a look of enchantment as they saw or felt new things. I was enchanted, too, when examining toes or fingers or tiny ears. Can you imagine ways that you might become enchanted with God in "all of life" when you become a mother? How can you be enchanted now while you wait for an adoption or birth?

Dear Father, I know there are lots of things I don't know about you. Help me remember that you are worthy of worship every moment of every day. Help me see you in all of life. Please grant me grace to worship you in spirit and in truth.

Day 5:
Overflowing Grace

*"Now the Lord is the Spirit, and where the Spirit of the Lord is,
there is freedom. And we all, with unveiled face,
beholding the glory of the Lord, are being transformed into
the same image from one degree of glory to another.
For this comes from the Lord who is the Spirit."*

2 Corinthians 3:17-18

My day begins, not because the sun is up, but because the pulsing cries of my child jolt me awake and demand that I crawl out of my warm bed. There is no snooze button. I'm tired because of forty nights of interrupted sleep, annoyed that my husband is still in bed catching zzz's, and frustrated that I didn't get to fold the pile of baby clothes crumpled in the rocker where I want to sit. I toss the clothes on the floor, pick up the baby, and flop in the chair. I bring a bottle to the screaming creature that I know issued from my body or that I purposefully chose in adoption, but *I'm not feeling the love.* Not this morning anyway. I realize I'm beginning the day badly. What do I do? How do I put on the brakes and back up? How can I fill my heart so I can serve my family in love?

Have you ever watched a flower unfold via time-lapse photography? The flower slowly, petal by petal, opens itself up to the sun until it's fully exposed to its light and warmth. Similarly, to live lives of fullness, we present ourselves to the Son, his Word, Spirit, and to the light and warmth of his grace. We allow his mercy to coax our clinched hearts open to his fullness. We slowly unfurl our sin, our pain, our frustration, and our longings, and we let each "petal" soak in the radiance of his glory and grace as seen scripture. We allow his love and forgiveness to beam upon us, we receive it by faith, and somehow we are transformed. It is a mystery.

When I look on my life, much of it has been lived on empty. I wanted to live out of a full heart but didn't know how. Mainly, I tried harder to do better, and that led to disappointment and anger with myself. *Now what I know is grace.* Hallelujah!

There is no checklist on how to be full of the Spirit for everyday life as a saved sinner. There are no set rules for perfect results. Desperation and dependence seem to open God's heart to our emptiness. Somehow, childlike faith in his ability to do what we can't is a key—not to perfection, but to a deep rest in the completed work of Christ. We trust in his sure but unpredictable grace at work in us through faith, a grace that is as sure as Christ's death and resurrection, and as certain as his faithful love. And as we wait with open hearts, he comes. This is grace.

1. How does the Spirit work to change your heart according to the above scripture?

2. In unfolding your life before God to let his light shine on you, what truth about God's character might help you most today? Use scripture.

Today, O Lord, I open up my heart of unbelief to your unfailing love and faithfulness. Help me remember your grace and mercy for this day. As I do, help me live out of the fullness of your firmly established grace toward me.

No Condemnation: A Mother's Day Sermon

[Matt Redmond is a pastor turned banker who has seen the ugly beautiful both inside the church and in the business world. His blog, mattbredmond.com, *addresses the intersection of real life and theology, but you can also count on him for a good laugh in* Thursday's Random Thoughts. *The following is a blog post he wrote in 2011.]*

As an associate pastor at a small church, one day I had a flash of fear. You see, I thought I was scheduled to preach on the quickly approaching Mother's Day. My blood ran cold as I was overcome with the peculiar fear of what to say and how to say it.

Wonder of wonders, it was an error. I realized I did not have to preach on that day. But the sermon was already forming, and here it is.

Usually one of three types of sermons is preached on Mother's Day. The first one is a celebration of mothers. You know the one: "Mothers are awesome! God loves mothers! Look at Mary!" The second tells mothers how to be better mothers. "Be like Mary or Hannah or . . . <insert biblical heroine here>." Basically: "Happy Mother's Day . . . now here is how to succeed at mothering." The third sermon we sometimes hear is one that has nothing to do with mothers. To be honest, this is the one I usually prefer. Honor the mothers . . . wait—all the women in the congregation and then preach on whatever you would have preached on if it were not Mother's Day.

So, I thought about it. How would I honor the mothers in the congregation? My words should be practical. Encouraging. And rooted in the heart of God for mothers. And they shouldn't be the vacuum-cleaner-as-a-gift kind of honoring. This is not a time for bitter medicine; it's a time for affirmation. Here's the outline:

Romans 8:1 says, "There is therefore now no condemnation for those who are in Christ Jesus." Mothers, if you are in Christ Jesus, you do not have to fear condemnation. You stand in the righteousness of Christ and are loved by God as his daughter because of Christ's work on your behalf on the cross.

Mothers, even though you may feel you are…

- *You are not condemned* by your messy home.
- *You are not condemned* by your lack of desire to homeschool.
- *You are not condemned* by your personal sins.
- *You are not condemned* by the difficulty of caring for a child with special needs.
- *You are not condemned* by the knowledge of how easy it is for you to love one child more than another.
- *You are not condemned* by your miscarriage(s).
- *You are not condemned* by your lack of desire to have more kids.
- *You are not condemned* because you have no desire to adopt.
- *You are not condemned*—even though you feel it—when you read of another's perfect parenting moment on Facebook.
- *You are not condemned* by your inability to cook.
- *You are not condemned* because your kids are not "normal."
- *You are not condemned* because you are divorced or unmarried and doing it alone.
- *You are not condemned* by your desire to be alone, away from the kids, for a time, every. single. day.
- *You are not condemned* by your body, which is not what it once was.

- *You are not condemned* by your repeated failures as a mother.
- *You are not condemned* by your rebellious children.
- *You are not condemned* by the frustration of having to scrape mac and cheese off the kitchen floor. Again.
- *You are not condemned* by all the fears and tears which flirt with insanity and take you to the precipice of despair.
- *You are not condemned* by not being able to throw the birthday party of the year for your kids.
- *You are not condemned* for not feeding your kids homemade meals whose ingredients were recently purchased at Whole Foods.
- *You are not condemned* by your need for a vacation. Without kids.
- *You are not condemned* because you cannot take your kids on exciting vacations.
- *You are not condemned* for not living up to the standards of your mother or mother-in-law.
- *You are not condemned* by the stares of those who don't have kids when yours erupt into volcanic screams in public places.

Mothers, even though you may feel condemned, if you are in Christ, you are not condemned. This is the real reality.

If you are in Christ, your identity as a sinner before a holy God is replaced with the righteousness of Christ alone. So go forward in freedom, with the unending affection and acceptance of being a daughter perfectly adored with an unwavering love that flows from your Father in Heaven.

Additional Encouragement for the Adoptive Mom

Carrie Brock and Lauren Kirkland

Dear adoptive mommy,

As moms with a new child in the home, many of the entries in this study apply to us. But as adoptive moms, we face additional and unique challenges. In the beginning, there is so much to be done in bringing your child to their forever home. For many, the next step is usually waiting, where there is *nothing to do except wait.* There are plenty of places where evil can attack us, including isolation, fear, guilt, and shame. Unknowns abound on the road to adoption, and both Lauren and I have experienced many of them. It may be that the questions you may have don't have answers—at least in this life. And not everyone around you can understand your heartaches and pains; sometimes you may not even understand them yourself. These feelings can be isolating and hard to explain.

Our hope is that these pages speak to those who are on that long and complex road of adoption, or in those intrepid first weeks at home. We hope you will use them in addition to the main study as encouragement for your specific spot. And be encouraged, you are not alone!

In adoption, there is not much expecting…because you don't really know *what* to expect. Adoption is indeed a journey to motherhood, but much of the journey is very different than having a biological child. Lauren and I have five adopted children between each of our families, and each adoption was unique with different challenges. For Lauren and I, walking the road together in friendship and support of one another has encouraged both of us in many ways, including knowing that we are not alone in this journey. We have found that stepping into community, with adoptive and biological mothers, offers great support, insight, and encouragement.

We pray that you will feel God encouraging you on your journey and see him providing comfort through his mercies, provision, and community. There is an Almighty God, a High Priest, who is with you every step of the way. Bring your questions, heartaches, pains, and desires to Him, your Abba Father. Put your hope in Him.

By his grace—for his glory,

Carrie

Week 2 Role Change:
The Deep End

*"If you abide in me, and my words abide in you,
ask whatever you wish, and it will be done for you.
By this my Father is glorified, that you bear much fruit
and so prove to be my disciples. As the Father has loved me,
so have I loved you. Abide in my love."*

John 15:7-9

Some people ease into the water from the stairs, slowly getting wet inch by inch. Others jump right in, getting completely wet. In an instant splash they are submersed in water. I am one of those who gently ease into the water. But with adoption, it seems to be a "jump-in-the-deep-end" experience.

It's hard to know what to expect—what will that water be like? The waiting becomes harder and longer than you thought it was going to be. Who is your child going to be? Where is your child now? There are similar wonderings, waiting, fears with pregnant mothers, but it is a different type of anticipation than that of adoptive moms. And many times, it is hard for others to understand the unusual and complex emotions involved in adoption: feelings of inadequacy, lies from Satan telling us anyone can have a baby, or fears of how bonding will take place when you're instantly thrust into motherhood. We don't have nine months of growing love for a baby tucked under our hearts. We must completely trust God to grow love in our hearts for the child he has in his hands for us. There is doubt: will I be enough? Am I good enough? Who will I become? Who do I need to be? But God knows our hearts, and he knows how to meet us. His arms are open to catch us as we jump into that deep water.

God calls us to abide in him because he knows that apart from Him, we can do nothing. The adoption process along with the first few days, weeks and months after Gotcha Day definitely call for abiding. Some of those days I just didn't abide and I tried to get by on my own. Those days didn't work out so well and didn't bear much fruit. It's hard to bear beautiful fruit when you have zero energy and lots of fear. But all we really need to do to is BE—be with God, be with our Lord—and he will allow us to bear much fruit—fruit for the world to see! And in this—through the joys and pains—He alone will be glorified.

1. Do you feel that you have jumped into the deep end?

2. What are the lies that Satan is whispering to you? Lies of failure? Of self-doubt?

Lord, let us see your true path for our lives, and may it give us perseverance and strength. We know your plan is the best plan—and we will follow you with our whole hearts. Let us hear your truth, and guard our hearts and minds from the lies of the evil one.

Week 2 Role Change:
The New Community

"For you did not receive the spirit of slavery to fall back into fear, but you have received the Spirit of adoption as sons, by whom we cry 'Abba, Father.' The Spirit himself bears witness with our spirit that we are children of God, and if children, then heirs—heirs of God and fellow heirs with Christ, provided we suffer with him in order that we may also be glorified with him."

Romans 8:15-17

When you embarked on the road of adoption, you may have blazed a trail that was new to your friends and family, or you may have known many others who were familiar with it. However, when you come into the "family" of adoption, it is a completely new community. It's one that I never thought I'd be a part of and one that I didn't know that I would be so passionate about. Some have this calling their whole lives, knowing that adoption will be part of their family story. Others find the road to adoption by a change in course. However you get there, adoptive moms are a community that understand the unique longings, waiting, pain, and abundant joys that come with the journey of adoption.

The unmet longing to birth your own child, waiting to hold your adopted child, and the desire to be there for those first few moments, days, months or even years with your child—is a burden that comes with adoption. When you see and feel the love you have for your adopted child, your eyes are opened to the way God loves us—and adopted us.

We call him *Father*, and we are his children. He called us to Himself. He also wants to give us everything—we are his heirs! How amazing! But that last part is harder: "we must also share his suffering." Adoptive moms may not have the pains of childbirth, but there are other pains and suffering to endure. But in the end—what joy we have!

Ecclesiastes 4:12 says, "Though a man might prevail

against one who is alone, two will withstand him—a threefold cord is not quickly broken."

You can get through the adoption process alone—or just with your spouse—but what a blessing to have those that have walked before you, and who walk alongside you during your adoption process. Those that can pray with you, grieve with you, wait with you, and even jump up and down with excitement with you—sharing in your intense longings and exceeding joys.

And as you take this journey with the Lord, remember this oh so important thing: he is there always—in every minute, every tear, every joy, and every pain.

1. Do you long for community with other adoptive families?

2. How has God revealed to you the picture of adoption? What does it mean to you that we are adopted into his family?

Heavenly Father, let me see your love for me as a father to a daughter. Let me feel the passion of adoption, as only you can give. Thank you for a community of women that will share this journey with me.

Week 3 Control:
Wanting and Waiting (and Waiting)

"In the six hundredth year of Noah's life, in the second month, on the seventeenth day of the month, on that day all the fountains of the great deep burst forth, and the windows of the heavens were opened."

Genesis 7:11

Have you ever felt like you were stuck in a place in life? Were you wondering how or why you got started down that path in the first place? While I was going through the waiting and the wanting process of adoption, I reread the story of Noah. Noah trusted and obeyed God before and through the flood—but after the rains, there was more waiting—and trusting to be done.

Genesis 7:17a says, "The flood continued forty days on the earth..." So forty days of the flood.

But then Genesis 8:3-5 says,

> And the waters receded from the earth continually. At the end of 150 days the waters had abated, and in the seventh month, on the seventeenth day of the month, the ark came to rest on the mountains of Ararat. And the waters continued to abate until the tenth month; in the tenth month, on the first day of the month, the tops of the mountains were seen.

That is almost ninety more days! *Months* after the rains, they came to rest – and stopped floating. I would have wanted to get off that boat right then, the second the floating was finished. But there was more waiting. It seems like there was just a tiny bit of progress in every stage of Noah's wait. Stopping on the mountain created a little more hope. They were closer to the goal but no dry land. Not yet.

Genesis 8:6, 10, 12-13a,14-16a says,

> At the end of forty days Noah opened the window of the ark that he had made ... He waited another seven days, and again he sent forth the dove out

of the ark. Then he waited another seven days and sent forth the dove, and she did not return to him anymore. In the six hundred and first year, in the first month, the first day of the month, the waters were dried from off the earth. In the second month, on the twenty-seventh day of the month, the earth had dried out. Then God said to Noah, "Go out from the ark..."

In adoption, many people find that there is so much waiting. And there is usually waiting and longing before the actual process even begins. There are so many unknowns and opportunities to trust where we have absolutely no control. Who will my child be? Trust in the Lord. The paperwork is lost. Trust. The wait increased (again). Trust. I want my family *now*. Trust. Wait. Watch. Listen.

1. Where do you see that God is in control—and will be faithful to you in your journey?

2. Where are the areas that you are still trying to control? Or where are you consumed with worry?

Lord, guard my heart for each day, week and moment of my waiting. Remind me that you are in control. Hold my longing heart in Your hands

Week 3 Control:
Fight the Lies

"There is no fear in love, but perfect love casts out fear. For fear has to do with punishment, and whoever fears has not been perfected in love."

1 John 4:18

From the beginning of my adoption journey, I felt joy and complete confidence that I was on the right path for me and my future family—God's path. But as the weeks and months passed, fear crept in and I heard the whisper of lies. *What if it never happens? What if you don't bond with your child? You aren't going to be good enough. It shouldn't be this hard.*

Some days the lies sounded like foolishness; it was easy to choose truth. But there were darker days when the lies made sense. Those were the days I had to cling to the promises of the Lord and his promises and to fight to see hope in a not-so-hopeful situation. Clinging to truth relieves the fear of the future—the fear that the lies might be valid. Many on the adoption journey suffer heartbreak while waiting: losing, longing, questioning. Whatever your pain is, God is in control. He sees the longing and the wounding that we hold deep in our hearts, and he will walk with us in every step, holding us and cradling our heart in his tender hands.

But the waiting and longing is only half the battle; once we bring our children home, there are even more lies. *Why haven't I bonded with my child yet? I didn't give birth. I shouldn't have postpartum baby blues. What if my child doesn't think of me as her real mom? What if I don't think of myself as her real mom?*

We have to seek the truth. We stop listening to the lies and trust that we are the perfect moms for our children. God designed it that way. God created them to be *our* children. We will give all the imperfect human love we have to our children, but the best love we can give them is to point them to the One that loves perfectly. He alone is the Way the Truth and the Life (John 14:6).

1. What lies are you hearing from the Deceiver?

2. What truths is the Lord telling you to cling to?

Dear Lord, give me wisdom to know that the lies ARE lies. Let me how you are in control and open my eyes to the hope that is in you. Drive fear out of my heart and fill me with your love.

Week 4 Perfectionism:
A Night Out Intro- Adoptive Mom Version

A night out with your husband, or even with friends may look very different for an adoptive mom. You may feel that it was too easy to leave. Or conversely, you may feel that it is too hard to leave, and are tempted to not leave at all. Maybe you are in a situation where you would really like a night out, but you can't leave for one reason or another. Whatever your circumstances, they can all make us feel guilty. We may feel like we haven't "earned it"—because our bodies have not been through childbirth. Or you may feel like you're really earned it—after all, you asked for this child, worked to bring this child home, prayed, begged, waited and wanted this child.

What's your poison? How are you attacked? Bring the specific lies you hear before your Heavenly Father and surrender them to his loving kindness.

If adopting an infant, you may still be in the bonding stages, and leaving will be harder for you than the baby. But if you have an older child freshly home, there will be other aspects of leaving the house that you may need to talk through with your family.

But we need this. To love our family, we have to take care of ourselves! Putting ourselves first on occasion is really choosing to put our families first—by giving them a refreshed, encouraged, connected mommy, who is ready to enter into the challenges and joys of motherhood.

Week 4 Perfectionism:
Chosen

> *"In love he predestined us for adoption as sons through*
> *Jesus Christ, according to the purpose of his will,*
> *to the praise of his glorious grace,*
> *with which he has blessed us in the Beloved.*
> *In him we have redemption through his blood,*
> *the forgiveness of our trespasses,*
> *according to the riches of his grace,*
> *which he lavished upon us, in all wisdom and insight*
> *making known to us the mystery of his will,*
> *according to his purpose, which he set forth in Christ*
> *as a plan for the fullness of time, to unite all things in him,*
> *things in heaven and things on earth."*
> Ephesians 1:4b-10

Chosen is one of my favorite words, especially in the context of adoption. Our kids were chosen to be ours by the holy God of the universe! And we are chosen to be HIS—we are chosen to be children of God. Every day in the faces of our children, we get to see the personification of adoption. However much we love and cherish our children and know that they are our children, how much more does our Abba Father love us and call us his own. We are adopted into his family, grafted in to his family tree. We are chosen to be His, just as he chose our children to be ours!

We do not demand perfection from our children to earn our love and neither does our Lord. We cannot be perfect . . . at all. And wondrously, he does not ask us to. However, as believers, we are made perfect by his love for us and by the blood of Jesus Christ.

Sometimes, sadly, we demand perfection from ourselves. I can believe the lie that I must be the perfect mom for my children. I have a desire to be everything they need, especially when I consider the difficult beginning that my children had in life. I want to be everything for them. But in God's wondrous goodness to me, every day that I seek to be perfect—I fail. And on the days that I seem to want it more, I fail even bigger than before. I have to realize, in my imperfection, I have been chosen for these children. And they have been chosen for me. And when I fail, I ask to be washed clean by the blood of The Perfect One and hope that I can point my children's focus toward him.

1. Is searching and striving to make things perfect for your child causing you grief and stress?

2. How can you begin to let go of these things?

Father, thank you for calling us your daughters. Help us strive for a heart of love and keep our minds on you. Let us seek Jesus and his perfection instead of striving for our own.

Week 4 Perfectionism:
The Plan

"For I know the plans I have for you, declares the Lord, plans for welfare and not for evil, to give you a future and a hope. Then you will call upon me and come and pray to me, and I will hear you. You will seek me and find me, when you seek me with all your heart."

Jeremiah 29:11-13

One day I got to a crossroads, and I asked, "Oh Lord, where do you want me to go?" I could travel farther down the road of fertility, but it didn't seem like the right path. I felt God leading somewhere else. He was leading to adoption. I never felt called to adoption, but I did feel a strong urge to go to an informational meeting to find out about other options—other possible paths that God might have for us. After that meeting, I knew. We knew. We were going to be adopting. God was showing us that this was *his* plan. His divine, wonderful, blessed, and full plan. It was so clear—and so unexpected!

When we were trying to start our family, I made a plan. I had basically written my plan and handed it to God. I was totally trusting God and believing in his power—to make the plan that I designed happen. But it was MY plan. I believed, but I wasn't ready to listen — not yet. As our journey for a family continued with unmet desires time and time again, I was wondering what had happened to my plan. I had trusted that God could do it. As adoption was revealed to us, I thought it would be a good "second choice." I began to trust God for his second best. I didn't realize at the time that it was a much better plan—a perfect plan full of abundant blessings. I had never imagined the blessings we would have through adoption.

As adoptive moms, we also have to deal with our expectations of how our adoption is going to be—or "should" be—versus the reality. Maybe we thought it would be different. Maybe we thought that if we just got home, on a schedule, or just something predictable—that everything would be okay. But there is often a long road before we actually feel like mothers.

God is with us when it doesn't go as planned. He is leading, and thankfully, He's completely in control! Seek him daily to see where he is leading. It may be somewhere you never thought you would go!

1. How has God shown you his perfect plan through your adoption journey—for your child and for other aspects of your life?

2. How can you seek encouragement and reject thoughts of failure when hope is waning and the future seems so far away?

Dear Lord, open our eyes to your perfect plan. Let us seek you with our whole heart, knowing that you want the very best for us, even if it is not what we have planned for ourselves. Please give us hope when we are hopeless and restore to us the peace that surpasses our understanding.

Week 5 Comparison:
What You Hear...

*"Rejoice in the Lord always; again I will say, rejoice.
Let your reasonableness be known to everyone.
The Lord is at hand; do not be anxious about anything,
but in everything by prayer and supplication with thanksgiving
let your requests be made known to God.
And the peace of God, which surpasses all understanding,
will guard your hearts and your minds in Christ Jesus."*

Philippians 4: 4-7

There are many questions and comments you will hear while you journey to build your family story through adoption. If you have struggled with infertility, there are many questions and comments you never imagined you would hear, including, "Don't worry about it; it will happen," or "Just adopt, then you will get pregnant." While usually well-meaning, the comments remind you of the gaping hole in your heart.

I was discouraged by the comments that I heard around me, as well as the things that I told myself. Seeing pregnant women around me, hearing successful stories of adoption, and feeling "abnormal" all broke my heart. The verses suggesting that I "rejoice in the Lord always" were a struggle—especially while I was longing for a child. I had made my requests known on so many occasions. What I truly felt in my heart was a desire and a calling to be a mother. But where was my child? I prayed, hoped, desired, and longed. Yet still, my arms were empty. I felt like a failure as a woman.

When my husband and I started to walk down the path of adoption, I had a joy and a peace that I had not had in a long time. I knew that we were on the right path, and that God knew who my child was. This peace was beyond understanding. There were many hard days, but I felt God leading still. Sharing with others about this new peace and trust strengthened my heart for adoption and deepened my faith in my wonderful, all-knowing, powerful, loving God!

However, comments from others don't end after you bring your child home. "Are they yours?" "Is one of them your real (meaning biological) child?" "Are they sisters/brothers?" In the wonderful grace story of families of every size, shape and color, there is God-given peace. And he gives words to speak and grace to know how to speak them to those that we encounter.

1. Are there things that you are hearing from yourself and others that are discouraging you?

2. What are some practical ways that you can fight to hear the words of your Father louder than hurtful comments from your flesh or from others?

Thank you Lord for your gift of peace. Fill us with your wisdom and grace to face the days ahead. Give us joy in our lives and peace beyond our understanding. Remove worry from our minds and instill in us calmness. Encourage us on this journey! Help us keep our eyes on you.

Week 5 Comparison:
Expectations

"For God alone, O my soul, wait in silence, for my hope is from him. He only is my rock and my salvation, my fortress; I shall not be shaken. On God rests my salvation and my glory; my mighty rock, my refuge is God."

Psalm 62:5-7

When you picture the children that you and your husband will have, you imagine certain aspects. Will they have his eyes and your hair? Will they have your husband's smile but your laugh? If you struggled with infertility, one of the things you may have longed for is that your children would look like you. But when you face adoption, you know that's not going to happen. As I joyfully started the journey to adopt, I accepted that my children were not going to look like us. But I also knew that I would love them as my own and that we would be connected—even if I didn't understand exactly how at the time. It's amazing to see how God often blesses even that part of adoption. Many children end up with attributes of their adoptive parents. God has a wonderful way of giving us our desires, even if they come wrapped in an unexpected package.

Society usually expects you to biologically bear your own children, and when you can't you wonder, "What is wrong with me?" You almost feel like you've failed as a woman. Thankfully, through adoption, God can heal the part of your heart that says something is wrong. Adoption brings with it a blessing that covers so much pain, and heals so much wounding. It brings an unconditional love and a special understanding of how God loves us.

So many people that we encounter don't understand the heart for adoption. I often feel like an adoption billboard—explaining how it works, how long we waited, how we brought our child(ren) home and everything in between. Adoption has been a wonderful opportunity to share the amazing things that God has done as he has moved and worked miracles. I even love sharing about the healing he has done on the deep wounds in my heart.

1. Where are the areas that you are struggling with comparison to other mothers—especially in the areas of adoption? Ask God to be faithful and gracious in your longings in this area.

2. Think about your story of adoption, your reasons and your calling. How God is moving in your life? Ask God to help you be ready to share with those that have questions and comments.

Lord, be with us during our journey of adoption. Give us strength and peace when we are sharing our story with others: our ups and downs, dreams and realities. Oh Lord, be our Rock that we can rest on when things just don't seem fair. Let us know that your glory will be seen in our lives!

Week 6 Loneliness:
Isolation for the Adoptive Mom

"God makes a home for the lonely; he leads out the prisoners into prosperity, only the rebellious dwell in a parched land."
Psalm 68:6 (NASB)

As a mom who has adopted two boys domestically, I have been privileged to bring my children into my home as infants. I work part-time, so I have several days at home with my kids and a couple of days at work. Upon returning to work after maternity leave, I often heard the comment, "I didn't even know you were pregnant!" While this is a natural assumption when someone returns from maternity leave, it made me feel separated from the "real moms" who gave birth. This is a lie that Satan tells me—that he tells us all.

Whether we stay at home or work outside the home, we will experience feelings of isolation at times because we are mothers, but we also experience them because we are *adoptive* moms. Satan's favorite trick is to make us feel alone, as if no one can understand what our struggles are. If your children are adopted domestically, people might ask you questions about pregnancy. They might also ask you if you could have had "children of your own". If you have children who are adopted internationally, people might stare at your unusual family, and they probably won't understand the emotional issues or adjustments that you and your children are experiencing.

Thankfully, we have a great High Priest who understands our weaknesses. And we have a God who loves adoption! He confirms it throughout his Word. Ephesians 1:5 speaks to God's heartbeat regarding adoption: "In love he predestined us for adoption as sons through Jesus Christ, according to the purpose of his will." Your children were chosen for you before the foundation of the world, and only YOU can be the best mom for them! When we feel lonely or misunderstood, we can cling to the promise that God equips those that he calls. "He who calls you is faithful; he will surely do it" (1

Thess. 5:24). We have a Father we can turn to. As we do we understand and know that we are not alone and that God has perfectly orchestrated our families.

1. What are the struggles that you are facing as an adoptive mom? In what ways do you feel lonely or isolated?

2. Our Savior experienced loneliness and isolation too. In what ways can we fight to believe the truths of scripture about our calling as moms?

Father, thank you that you adopted us into your family and gave us a beautiful picture for our children! Thank you that you are the perfect parent. Please equip us to love our children well and cause us to believe that your strength is made perfect in our weakness.

Week 6 Loneliness:
I am a Rock. I am an Island.

"Be strong and courageous. Do not fear or be in dread of them, for it is the Lord your God who goes with you. He will not leave you or forsake you."

Deuteronomy 31:6

"I am a rock, I am an island. And a rock feels no pain; And an island never cries."

Paul Simon

I love that song—I especially loved it in high school during seasons of emotional angst! I revisited these lyrics when I was going through infertility and in the beginning of the adoption process. I felt so alone. I felt that there was no one that understood. I saw everyone around me having babies and baby showers. Then they were going on to have a second child, and there I was, still childless. I felt that I had to close off and build walls so that no one would see the hurt and pain. The depth of pain was too much for other people – and too much for me. I avoided conversations that would cause me pain, or situations where I might be exposed in my loneliness. I felt alone. I became the island.

Through prayer and listening to the words of God, I started the healing process. I wasn't alone; God was with me. God had a plan for me and he was restoring me. As I looked around I found that there were others that were on similar paths. They also felt alone, and it made me not feel so alone anymore! Jesus understands our loneliness: he was alone many times, and people didn't understand what he was doing and why he was doing it. He is with us and knows how our loneliness feels. The Great Comforter will draw near to us!

The adoption process from start to finish is not what I planned for my life. And it is not what I thought it would be or what I thought it *should* be. It is a roller coaster of good and bad, and many times there are extremes on both ends.

The longings that you had for birth children may not come to fruition, but God builds new dreams while we are on the journey. God is with us. He will guide us, be with us, hold us, and comfort us.

1. Do you see how God is molding your heart and allowing you to see the path down which he is leading you?

2. Are there walls of protection that you need to ask Christ to break down in order to allow healing to begin?

Father, heal our wounded hearts. Bring us together with others so that we know that we are not alone. Wrap us in your loving arms so that we feel healed and restored as we journey on this path to which you have called us. Let us feel your strength so that we do not feel alone.

About the Contributors

Holly Mackle *writes, gardens, and does not correct the phrase "eddybody, eddywhere" in Birmingham, Alabama. She is wife to David and mama of two flower-sneaking bitties. Holly blogs at diggingsuburbia.com.*

Linda Barrett *writes, paints, and teaches Bible classes in Birmingham, Alabama. She is mother to three grown children and wife of one kind man. Linda blogs at invitationtowonder.wordpress.com*

Dr. Jenn Hale *is a practicing physician and competitive swimmer who loves to write in her spare time. She is wife to Heath and mommy to two beautiful little girls, Aliena and Emaleigh. She lives, works, and worships in Birmingham, Alabama.*

Jessica Hale *lives in Birmingham, Alabama with her husband Justin and their three little ones. When she's not corralling kids, she enjoys drinking coffee, reading, and exercising.*

Brandie Wolfe *loves biographies, documentaries, and interior decorating. She resides as the Queen of her house, being the wife to Jason and mommy to her two little tender warriors.*

Carrie Brock *loves coffee, gray skies and rainy days but is scared of storms. She enjoys being creative, both in writing and crafting. And she finds organizing very relaxing. She and her husband have their quiver full with three adopted kids.*

Lauren Kirkland *is a speech pathologist, wife to her college sweetheart, and mama to two sweet, rambunctious boys. She loves losing herself in a good book, music, and the outdoors, especially the beach.*

Endnotes

[1] RC Sproul, *Truths We Confess: A Layman's Guide to the Westminster Confession of Faith: Vol. 1* (Phillipsburg: P&R, 2006), 107.

[2] John Piper, Brothers, *We Are Not Professionals* (Nashville: Broadman and Holdman, 2002), 232.

[3] Piper, Brothers, *We Are Not Professionals*